A YOUTH FORUM BOOK

YOU WANT TO CHANGE THE WORLD?

SO CHANGE IT!

by Paul Simon

THOMAS NELSON INC.

New York / Camden

Library of Congress Catalog Card Number: 73–147917
International Standard Book Number: 0–8407–5314–4
Printed in the United States of America

Foreword

This book is one of a series in a unique publishing effort in which Youth Research Center, Inc., Minneapolis, Minnesota, has joined with Thomas Nelson Inc., Camden, New Jersey. The books are based on the very real concerns, problems, aspirations, searchings and goals of young people today as measured by nation-wide surveys being conducted continuously by the research center.

Central to the series is the belief that we all have a compelling need to turn to a core of faith for guidelines in coping with the world in which we live. Each book deals with a specific need or concern of young people viewed in relation to the Christian faith. By drawing upon the results of the surveys, each author is helped to speak more directly to the conflicts, values and beliefs of today's young people.

The significance of this series is enhanced, as well, by the scholarship and commitment of the authors. The grasp of the field in which each writes lends authority to their work and has established this series as a basic reference eagerly read and appreciated by young people.

Dedication

To a former United States Senator, Paul H. Douglas, who has inspired untold numbers of young people to take an active part in our political process. His example has meant more to me than he will ever know.

Contents

YOU WANT
TO CHANGE
THE WORLD?

SO CHANGE IT!

1.

Needed: Change in "the System" Question: Can You Change It?

The year was 1970.

Cambodia. Kent State. Jackson, Mississippi.

All three were on the minds of students in high schools and colleges across the nation and the world.

Hoping to keep campus violence to a minimum, and to try to move toward some long-range solutions, I called the student government leaders of the 13 largest universities in Illinois to my apartment in Springfield.

All those invited were present, and for almost three hours I mostly listened to the conversation. Most of us were sitting on the living room floor because my small apartment did not have anywhere near 33 chairs. When people—whether in their twenties or eighties—sit on a living room floor, somehow the conversation is frank. It's hard to be phony when you're sitting on the floor.

What I heard was not too different from talk I have heard on many campuses. Cambodia and Kent State and Jackson accentuated and deepened the tone, but the message was the same. Young people see the ills which plague mankind today, and they want to cure those ills, or at to least try. For many young people, the image presented by their parents, by their school, by their church, and by public officials is indifference to these ills and a stubborn defense of the status quo.

There always have been defenders of the status quo, and there always have been those who wish to change things. But never before have so many young people been away from home, where the re-thinking and reevaluating process almost inevitably is speeded up. Never before have so many been trained to question and think, both at the high school and college level. Never before have so many people in a nation enjoyed the abundance that the citizens of the United States do today, but the children of these citizens examine that abundance and frequently find it meaningless.

Talk of the struggles of the depression years means something to parents but not to young people, unless they have read the recent best-seller, *Hard Times*, by Studs Terkel. My friend, Father Paul Asciola, suggests that for the first time we have a highly-trained generation of young people, but a generation afflicted with "historical amnesia."

Whatever the reasons—some bad, but more of them good—young people today are demanding change.

This book is directed to those of you who are so much a part of our today and tomorrow. It is about change and how you can most effectively achieve it. A book is somehow impersonal, but I hope you will consider this message personal.

I'm typing this portion with the television on in the background; my 9-year-old daughter and 6-year-old son are watching it. Like many other fathers, I see them lying comfortably on the living room floor laughing at some cartoon characters. And yet, while they are happy, I am concerned about their future. I know that in the next few years major decisions will be made by you which will alter their lives and those of other children all over the face of the earth.

I have much at stake in the decisions you may make as you read this book, so you will understand why this is a personal appeal to you to help achieve change in a responsible, effective way.

ARE WE HEADED FOR A VIOLENT REVOLUTION?

These next few pages are being typed in a little village in Guatemala called Huehuetenango. My wife and I and two children are spending our vacation in Central America. By chance today I have met three United States citizens, each different and yet all much alike.

Dr. R. Wendell Vance is a physician from Provo, Utah. I would guess his age at 62. His hair is gray and his physical appearance, though robust, indicates clearly that he is not part of the Now generation. Dr. Vance is a member of the Church of the Latter Day Saints (Mormons) and he is volunteering one month of medical service for a near-by village of Indians who otherwise would have no medical help. He sees the need for change and is willing to do something concrete to effect change. He considers himself a conservative politically, but defending the status quo is not enough for him.

John Cowden and Mard Naman have just graduated from high school in Santa Cruz, California. Two weeks after graduation they took off for Mexico and Guatemala, roughing it and getting by on a lot less than the traditional $5 a day. John is going to study either history or sociology at the University of California. Mard plans to attend a school sponsored by the Friends (Quakers) in New York and is not sure what he wants to do. Both are about 18; they are bright and intense, and they see the world in which they live with open eyes. They see the need for change, and they want to help bring it about. Responsibly. They are not radicals but I sense that they could be radicalized if they felt government was not taking the necessary steps to meet the needs of desperate people at home, in Mexico, in Guatemala, and elsewhere. They want change, and they are willing to sacrifice to help bring it about.

The physician and the two students represent the hope that a better world can be built. But it is by no means certain that a better world *will* be built. (In speaking about "a better world," I am not talking about some wild scheme for a Utopia. I am stating my belief that, without changing the nature of man, his tendencies to violence can be controlled, and the extremes of poverty and hopelessness can be drastically diminished.)

George Romney, a member of President Nixon's cabinet, recently said that the United States is "inching toward revolution." He meant violent revolution. In recent years, there has been more talk about revolution than at any time since the Great Depression of the 1930's.

A balancing outlook is that of a distinguished American historian who says we have become a nation with a case of hypochondria, and that despite our obsession with ailments we are basically healthy. You don't need to buy his thesis completely to believe this advice to be sound: "Unless we begin to believe that we won't be dead before morning, we may not be up to the daily tasks of a healthy life." *

While there is some validity to his theory, I find his anal-

* Daniel J. Boorstin, "A Case of Hypochondria." *Newsweek*, July 6, 1970.

ysis of hypochondria partially off the mark. I hesitate to accept it fully, not because of any insights I have into "the big picture," but because of little things. In college audiences I have addressed, a few students have advocated violent revolution. They represent a small minority of students, it is true, but 10 years ago almost no student advocated violence. This thinking is not confined only to large universities. In speaking at Bluffton College in Bluffton, Ohio —a fine Mennonite school—I heard the same refrain from one of the students. When this message reaches Bluffton, it cannot be ignored. This reaction on the part of some students—and sometimes non-students—might be categorized generally as coming from the Left, though many who advocate violent revolution are so totally without a program that it is difficult to identify them with any political philosophy.

The threat of violent revolution, however, comes not only from the Left.

Following the Kent State deaths, many Illinois campuses were in turmoil, as were others throughout the nation. In two Illinois communities, men who were thought of as civic leaders talked seriously about "taking the law into our hands to clear up this situation." The tone was ominous; these were people who believed that our system of government had failed to establish law and order. The prosecuting attorney of one county described how close we had come to violence from the Right: "We teetered on the brink of having a vigilante movement, backed overwhelmingly by public opinion in our county."

People in South Carolina who overturned a school bus carrying children to a court-ordered integrated school may not have been consciously using the phrase, "violent revolution," but they were practicing it.

I think of a man I met on the streets of LaGrange, Illinois, an attractive, moderate-to-high-income suburb near Chicago. I was campaigning for my present office of lieutenant governor. He appeared to be about 55 years old, well-dressed, the picture of respectability. I explained my candidacy for office and then had a brief but grim conversation with him which he ended with the emphatic words, "What America needs today is a good dictator!"

Whether the violent threat to change through orderly process is from the Left or the Right, the result could be the end of the traditional freedoms we enjoy, including this one I now use in writing out for you what I believe.

The lesson of history is clear: When people are faced with a choice of liberty with chaos, or order without liberty, they always choose the latter.

The criticism leveled against youthful leaders today, that they have no sense of history, I believe has some justification. This is understandable, for when I was 16 to 19 years old, I had little historical perspective, either. The difference is that leadership has been thrust upon today's young people, whether you want it or not, and if you lose your historical perspective, it might be easy to reach for immediate goals which could bring long-range calamity.

Are we headed toward suppression of freedom? Or toward a violent revolution?

The answer cannot be spelled out precisely, for none of us knows the future.

But if there are enough people like Dr. R. Wendell Vance, the volunteer physician, and if there are enough young people like John Cowden and Mard Naman willing to work hard and responsibly for a better world, we can approach the future with some hope.

Can the System Respond to Need, Bring Change?

Several weeks ago I had the chance to listen to an amazing young man, Ralph Nader. I had never heard him before and he impressed me.

A few years ago Nader did not own a car, but he strongly believed that automobiles should be made safer. Fifty thousand highway deaths in the United States each year appalled him. So he decided to fight General Motors, the largest corporation in the world with a yearly budget larger than the budget of most nations of the world. He also tackled Ford, Chrysler and American Motors, three gigantic corporations.

Who won?

Nader won. The public won. If you or your parents are driving a 1969 car, or a later model, that car is safer today, and hundreds, perhaps thousands, of lives have been saved because of Ralph Nader.

In the long run, the very corporations which resisted the changes will benefit by them.

Ralph Nader did not win every fight in his struggle with the auto manufacturers: he is not winning every fight he has launched against pollution, corporate structures, nursing home abuses, and other ills in our society. But he is winning many battles, and he no longer fights alone. Hundreds of volunteers are helping him, either full- or part-time.

Despite some weaknesses in the present political system, this conclusion is called for: *Any system which permits one solitary individual, armed with the facts and in the right, to triumph over the world's largest corporations has to have something essentially good about it.*

You could scarcely have found a less likely person to influence government policy than Dave Saunders. Dave lost many of the rights most of us enjoy. While serving a sentence in an Illinois state penitentiary for a murder committed when he was 17, Dave wrote to me about state policy on prison discharges. I served then in the state legislature and knew nothing about the facts. Dave told me that prisoners who had friends and relatives waiting to help them, and who had jobs waiting for them, were paroled. Parole agents then helped them adjust to civilian life. But those who had no friends and relatives, who had no jobs waiting, were given $25 and a suit of clothes and shoved out into the cold with no help. He wrote that this latter group needed help the most.

A check of the facts showed him to be correct. I then introduced a bill, which passed the legislature, giving prisoners to be discharged "conditional release," releasing them 90 days early and giving them assistance and supervision. This has greatly helped many men who have enough strikes against them already, and it all came about because one prisoner sat down and wrote a letter. (Incidentally, Dave is out now, married, and holding a responsible job with a university.)

You probably have heard that, traditionally, freshmen legislators listen and do not speak, and that legislative bodies are tradition-bound. In Illinois the legislature had so tied itself to archaic rules that it badly needed restructuring to bring it up-to-date. A freshman legislator, Representative Harold Katz, violated the rules of tradition. He sponsored a bill calling for a commission to take a good look at legislative procedures. The result: substantial improvement in legislative procedures that supposedly were unchangeable—and brought about by a talented freshman legislator.

The war in Vietnam has seemed to mushroom endlessly, with its growing toll of both civilian and military casualties.

Young people have sensed the moral dilemma and the need for a change in policy. But how do you change a policy backed by the leadership of both political parties and by a majority of public opinion? In 1968 Senator Eugene McCarthy and Senator Robert Kennedy campaigned for the Democratic nomination for the presidency, and for a reappraisal of foreign policy. The first test came in New Hampshire, and contrary to all polls and predictions, the McCarthy forces won over the supporters of Lyndon B. Johnson. Young people had gone to New Hampshire and had worked hard. Some had to shave ("clean for Gene"); many traveled long distances. They stuffed envelopes, licked stamps, answered phones. They walked from door-to-door, explaining their views, and they convinced enough people in one small state to shake the nation.

These young people helped force a modification and a reappraisal of policy. True, the change did not go as far as they wanted, but most observers agree they were primarily responsible for the shift in policy which halted the bombing of North Vietnam. The President hastened an announcement that he would not seek re-election. And the war in Vietnam started on its way to an eventual defusing —at least so it appears as this is being written. These young people who were willing to act and not just talk made a major impact on a difficult world problem.

It is too early to make historical judgments, but no one who writes the history of the decade just past can ignore the role these young people played in shaping world events. In fact, the role of young people has been significant enough to reach the pages of the sober, prestigious, and influential magazine, *Foreign Affairs*, which recently carried an article by a student, Steven J. Kelman, on "Youth and Foreign Policy." No such article would have appeared 10 years ago. Today young people play an important part in both domestic and foreign policy.

Ron Lawrence, in his twenties and married, learned almost by accident of some adoption practices going on in Illinois. Babies literally were being bought and sold. He contacted his state representative who checked into the matter, discovered that Ron was correct and introduced a bill calling for the creation of an Adoption Laws Commission. Federal officials told commission members that Illinois was the center for a black market in babies. The commission recommended a new state adoption code, which stopped the practice. All of this began with a young man who was concerned, and did something about it.

The point is not simply that young people can help change policy, but that action of any citizen—young or old —can have the same impact.

Montgomery, Alabama, has given us an example of how both young and old can work together. Many have heard of the Montgomery bus boycott which brought Dr. Martin Luther King to national prominence. On December 1, 1955, after a hard day's work Mrs. Rosa Parks, 42, seated herself in the "white section" of a city bus. When a white man entered and wanted her seat, the driver ordered her to give it up. Understandably, she refused. The police arrested her and the black population of Montgomery backed her with a boycott of the buses. That incident attracted national attention. Less well-known is the fact that in March of 1955, a similar incident in Montgomery had involved 15-year-old Claudette Colvin, and police had arrested her. That had angered the black community, and seven months later Mrs. Parks' refusal to move was "the straw that broke the camel's back." In reality, both 15-year-old Claudette and 42-year-old Mrs. Parks joined in breaking a law and a tradition which were an injustice for great numbers of people.

Many other illustrations could be given.

I have a special reason for knowing the system can respond to change and that young people can help effect change. Three times I have faced difficult political campaigns during which seasoned political observers counted me out. All three times I won, and young people who volunteered to "do the impossible" provided the balance.

In my first race for public office as a state representative, the leadership of my party had unanimously endorsed my opponent in the primary. But 46 students donated at least one full Saturday to go from door-to-door in my behalf, and we won. In a very real sense, whatever contributions I have made in the state of Illinois are a tribute to 46 young people who paid no attention to all those who assured them we had no chance of winning.

My hope, however, is that your primary interest would not be candidate-oriented, but issue-oriented. Generally, Americans find it easier to work for a person than a cause. Obviously the two are related, but young people who take an interest in a specific issue will find—frequently to their surprise—that the political system *can* respond.

That response may not come easily, but in no important field do you expect a quick and easy response. If Dr. Jonas Salk had given up after his first failures, we might not have a polio vaccine today. The person who is willing to keep on trying, through failures as well as successes, will find that the present political structure can be used to bring about healthy change.

This is not to suggest that the system is perfect. Changes are needed, but anyone, young or old, who is willing to dedicate himself to changing something by working through the present system will be surprised at how much can be accomplished.

You may find it hard to believe this next statement, but it is true: *I know of no one who has genuinely tried to influence government policy, and has been willing to work at it, who has not been at least partially successful.*

A high school senior who read the rough draft of this manuscript, wrote at this point: "I *do* find it hard to believe."

I can understand the disbelief.

But my statement still happens to be true. And it includes you.

Does That Mean Change Is Not Needed?

Absolutely not.

There are some things you should help change. The basic difficulty with the decision-making process now is that it responds more to pressure than to need. In a guest lecture at the Air Force Academy in Colorado, I used this example:

If a major utility in Colorado asks for a rate increase which would cost the citizens of the state $2 million a year (a relatively small rate increase), and at the same time a legislative bill asked $100,000 for more educational help for the Mexican-Americans in Colorado, which of the two is more likely to be approved? The answer in almost every state probably would be the same: the utility increase.

One of the reasons for many of today's disturbing headlines is that government has responded to pressure rather than need. The 12 people who write to a legislator about a problem are more likely to get attention than 1,200 desperately poor people who don't even know the legislature is in session, or who their legislators are. And so the needs of the 1,200 grow and grow and sometimes explode.

It is not only the poor who lose in this process. Sometimes middle income families are overwhelmed with problems, but because they own a small home and have a reasonable income they are not eligible for government help. Here is an actual example; only the name is changed. John Green is a retired carpenter who will be 73 years old. He and his wife saved their money during their working years and bought a small home. They also managed to put about $4,000 in the bank. They now live on social security of about $130 a month. They have two daughters, one married and with four children of her own and the other single and suffering from a bone disease which requires frequent hospitalization. Mr. and Mrs. Green have lost their $4,000 and, because of hospital bills of more than $2,700, they will have to sell their home. They are heartbroken but they have no choice.

The Greens have no lobbyist in their state capitol. They don't buy tickets to $100-a-plate dinners and so they have no special access to important decision-makers. No one considers them civic leaders. They write to someone in government asking for help, but not expecting it. For them government is some foreign creature, distant, remote, and not interested in their problems.

Compare them with Thomas White, president of a large corporation or labor union. His lot is not easy, either. Complicated problems face him daily and he works many more than the traditional 40 hours a week. But when he has special problems involving government, he can call the mayor, a congressman, a senator, and talk to him on a first-name basis. In addition, he has lobbyists in the state capitol and in Washington. He does not get everything from government that he wants, but he understands clearly how things work and he frequently is able to make them work for himself and his corporation.

Tom White should be able to follow government action

closely, know what is going on, and have a voice in government policies. But Mr. and Mrs. Green should, also. Now their voice is not nearly as strong as it should be. The same is true of most of the Mr. and Mrs. Greens, whether they live in a ghetto or on a farm, in a suburb or a small town, next to a service station or near a factory.

If government had been responding more to need than to powerful special interests, many of the housing, educational, employment, and crime problems which now face us would have been greatly reduced.

You ask, "If it is true that government responds too much to pressure rather than to need, what can be done about it?"

One step that is vital is to *change the system of financing political campaigns.* A campaign for the governorship of New York or California costs more than $5 million. A friend of mine ran for governor in another state on a budget of $3.5 million. A race for governor of Illinois calls for a *minimum* budget of $2 million. A recent candidate for New York's house of representatives spent $261,000.

Is there anything wrong with this kind of expenditure?

Several things.

First, there is the obvious tendency to make politics more and more an arena for the wealthy or the beholden.

Second, there is usually an imbalance in expenditures, and the candidates do not have an equal chance to present their cause to the public.

Third, those who have the money to help finance campaigns end up with more access to and influence with policy-makers than does the average citizen.

Let's deal with these last two in more detail.

In 1920 there were two candidates for president of the United States: Warren G. Harding and James Cox. Harding was opposed to the United States joining the League of Nations, the organization brought into existence by President Woodrow Wilson in an effort to bring peace among nations. The Harding-Cox campaign came in 1920, immediately after World War I, "the war to end all wars." Harding opposed joining the League, Cox favored it. Harding won and Cox lost. The failure of the United States to join the League probably caused its eventual collapse and helped pave the way for World War II. Many things could have prevented World War II, but one of them might have been a strong League of Nations.

During the 1920 election campaign, the Harding forces spent approximately $6 million and the Cox forces about $1 million. What if Harding and Cox had both had the same amount to spend? Would Cox have won? Would we have joined the League of Nations? Would we have prevented World War II?

We don't know the answers, but the most casual study of history shows that the great human tragedies are not suddenly created by evil men. They are built—brick by brick—by men and women of good intentions who neglect taking the little steps for good which ultimately lead to the big things.

A host of other illustrations could be used, many from the state and district where you who read these lines live. *Whenever one candidate has more money to spend than another candidate for the same office, there is a distortion of the democratic process.* Our system of government assumes that both candidates have an equal chance to present their cause to the public. If one candidate for the state senate spends $20,000 and the other spends $10,000, the candidate with twice the funds obviously has a distinct advantage, and that advantage usually does not come because of dedication to serving the public interest.

In addition to this factor of imbalanced expenditures,

another problem is the excessive influence that people who contribute to campaigns have almost automatically. This is not because of any secret or illegal deals such contributors make with candidates.

"But," you ask, "if there are no secret deals, what harm is done? You wouldn't do something wrong for someone who requested it, simply because he contributed to your campaign, would you?"

No, I would not, nor would most office-holders. But some problems remain. Here are two practical illustrations:

When I ran for lieutenant governor of Illinois, my campaign committee spent $108,000—a modest sum for any state-wide office in a major state. I am understandably grateful to those who contributed to that campaign, whether the contribution was small or large. (We were fortunate in receiving $27,000 in small contributions, an unusually high percentage.) Without those contributions I would not have had a chance.

But let's assume that tonight I get home about midnight, tired from a day of facing problems and probably a speech or two, also. I find messages awaiting me from 20 people who insist that it is important that I call each of them— and to each person, his problem is the most important. If I am to get any sleep, and if I am to be able to work reasonably well the next day, I can't return 20 phone calls. I might be willing to make one. Of the 20 who left messages for me to call, 19 are people whose names mean nothing to me, whom I do not recall having met or corresponded with. The 20th name is someone who sent me a $100 campaign contribution. Which call do you think I'll make?

You're right!

Without doing anything dishonest, the elected official feels a special debt of gratitude to those who contribute to his campaign. Rarely can such a contributor directly dictate a course of action by a public official, but he does have greater access to the public official than the average citizen. This means that those who have the financial ability to support campaigns have a greater voice in public policy than those who cannot afford to contribute.

Here is another practical example of the way campaign contributions influence public officials: In my first race for the Illinois house of representatives the experts believed I did not have a chance, and those who contributed to my campaign were few and far between. Two years later, when I looked like a "shoo-in" for reelection, more people suddenly took an interest in my campaign deficit. One group came to me and said they "liked young men in politics" and had decided to contribute $300. I checked the record and on 27 out of 29 votes important to this group, I had opposed them. They said their contribution would be "with no strings attached." They meant it in the sense that they did not want to commit me to any specific votes on any issue. But in reality there is no such thing as a contribution with "no strings attached," because you feel a sense of obligation to those who contribute. (Frankly, this is one reason I like fund-raising dinners, because those who come generally expect only to help a candidate, eat a dinner, and hear a speech. The small contributor generally is interested in good government.) Let us assume that I had accepted that contribution—which I did not—and let's say that I voted on every one of those measures exactly as I did in the previous session. During the floor debate, would I be as free to support vigorously a bill they opposed, or strenuously oppose a measure they supported? If their contribution had secured only silence from me instead of debate, it would have been a "good" investment.

In 1907 President Theodore Roosevelt sent a special

message to congress calling for a change in the financing of campaigns. We have done almost nothing since then to improve things, and the cost of campaigns has risen dramatically.

What's the answer?

There is no simple, easy, dramatic answer to this complicated problem—there are simple answers to few problems —but among the things which must be considered are these:

1. A certain amount of free radio and television time should be allotted to all major candidates. This could be considered part of the public service requirement of a radio or TV station.

2. While they are difficult to police, realistic restrictions must be imposed on the amount which can be spent in a campaign.

Unfortunately, a bill which would have restricted expenditures on radio and television to seven cents per vote cast in the last election—the only major reform in decades —was vetoed by President Richard Nixon.

3. There should be a periodic report on the amounts spent, with general information as to sources. This should be made not only after a campaign, but two or three times during a campaign. Some states require this now.

4. Serious consideration must be given to moving toward severe limitations on expenditures, with government paying for the amounts spent. The taxpayers pay now, in ways that generally do not benefit them, and they are not aware of it. They pay now because contributors often get their "pound of flesh" in return for their generosity. This usually is costly to the taxpayers directly; indirectly, it is costly because the people's real needs often are neglected while the

contributors' wishes are satisfied. If this change were effected, the public official would have a clear obligation to all citizens, not just to the financially fortunate few.

Besides working for these changes, you can help right now by contributing a small amount—even a dollar can be important—to a candidate in whom you believe. Your dollar will help him, and it will be a gentle reminder that the people to be served are not just the big contributors.

In states, and in some communities, an office of ombudsman should be created. Government too often responds to powerful pressures. And sometimes it does *not* respond, either for average citizens or for pressure groups.

Government is becoming increasingly complicated and there should be an office or agency able to cut the bureaucratic red tape and get something done.

The office of ombudsman—or complaint officer—has been created in Hawaii, Nebraska and Oregon. In Illinois the lieutenant governor's office now voluntarily performs this function. Many cities and universities also have created the office, as have some industrial plants. The term, "ombudsman," is Swedish and applies to an office, now common in many countries, which tries to help the average citizen with problems involving the government.

In the Scandinavian tradition, the ombudsman is primarily an investigator checking into abuses which have been charged against a governmental agency or official. In the United States, the office is much more of a service office which helps people who don't know where to turn as they face "this monster called government," which frequently does not seem to be *their* government in time of need.

Perhaps 90 percent of governmental decisions today are administrative decisions from which there is no court appeal. The understandable tendency for those in charge of any department is to back up the people under them. That means if someone applies for assistance to the health department in Jones county, and a clerk there says the person is not eligible, that clerk is likely to be backed up by the top person in the county office, then the top person in the regional office, and then the top person in the state office. This backing-up process is somewhat understandable because employees must feel their superiors have confidence in them, and those in charge of any office do not have time to review every decision in great detail.

But somewhere there must be a congressman, a legislator —or an ombudsman—who will ask the top person in a department to review a case and make sure that a review does take place.

Sometimes people take their problems to Agency A, which refers them to Agency B, which refers them to Agency C, which refers them back to Agency A. Someone has to help the citizen caught in this kind of run-around.

Here are some actual cases in Illinois from the most recent report on ombudsman activities:

A farmer had contended for some time that his land had been improperly replatted when a new highway came through. He had been unsuccessful in his efforts to have any agency look at the site. At our request, a highway department official reexamined the scene and agreed the man was right. The proper corrections were made on the records and the man has his land back.

An elderly man advanced money toward the burial expense of his brother who had died while receiving public aid. The funeral director was to reimburse the man after the state agency paid the funeral bills. The mortuary neglected to do so, despite numerous pleas from the man. He wrote to us. At our request, the state agency notified the funeral home that it would be removed from an approved list maintained by the department unless reimbursement was made immediately. They paid quickly.

We have become more and more aware that government too often is slow to respond to people's problems. Needs sometimes are immediate, but government is not geared to instant response.

A woman from a small southern Illinois town was without food or heat for her children because of a delay in the mailing of a public aid check. Her need was immediate. She had literally nothing for a cold week-end. She could not wait until Monday for her check. We contacted a local church which delivered groceries to her and gave her a small amount of money to see her family through the week-end.

Many long-range problems are brought to us. Two counties in southern Illinois have low income from tax revenue because a federal forest has removed so much land from their tax rolls. Legislators in the area have started to review possible legislative remedies.

An examination of the long-range economic difficulties caused by strip mines in some 26 counties in the state also is underway.

A rural township with 12,000 population—99 per cent black—in northern Illinois has every possible need. The community elders had banded together to raise $70,000 for a supermarket—the first in the community—and had the shell of the building completed when they were unable to secure additional financing which had been promised. Through our office, we helped find private financing to complete the building and stock it, with final details still pending. We also organized a task force headed by a volunteer, a Chicago attorney. He and other volunteers are helping the people try to secure adequate roads, sewer facilities, public health services, and industry. The people of this township have not asked for handouts. They seek only advice and direction. Among their major needs have been medical care and a community center. Under the attorney's leadership, the township learned how it could get matching federal funds for a medical center and a community center. A vote was held and the residents overwhelmingly approved a small tax for the project. We hope that one of the results will be that this community for the first time will have full-time medical help.

In Chicago there are perhaps 400,000 Spanish-speaking citizens of Mexican and Puerto Rican background. They have no direct representation in the Chicago City Council or in the legislature. We have worked with their leaders to ease some immediate personal problems. We have awakened the interest of the state's universities in this ethnic group, which has the highest school drop-out rate of any in the state. And we are exploring ways of meeting some of the immediate, pressing needs of the community.

Government is not going to get smaller. As our population grows and problems become more complex, government also will grow and become more complex. Creating the office of ombudsman will help make government more responsive to the needs of its citizens.

The problems of corruption must be faced candidly.

The theory of our government is that various interests and opinions collide, and that after public debate those who must make the decision—in the city council, state legislature or congress—cast their votes on the basis of the evidence presented to them.

For all of its difficulties, that system can work reasonably well if decisions are arrived at freely. But when there is money under the table to any of these officials, the free system obviously has been prostituted.

A few years ago a Louis Harris poll showed that more than 60 per cent of the American public believe that most public officials are corrupt. An opinion poll conducted among more than 11,000 high school students by the *Daily Citizen* of Tucson, Arizona, asked this question: "Do you have confidence in the integrity and competence of our city officials?" The answer: yes, 28.9 per cent; no, 49.5 per cent; no opinion, 21.4 per cent.

It would be comforting to believe that this opinion is typical only of Tucson but, sadly, we know otherwise. A high school senior in Illinois told me that a similar poll in his high school would show significantly worse results.

Fortunately, the reality is much better than the public image, though opinion is important because it reflects public confidence in governmental decisions. The majority of public officials do not violate any laws on bribery, and an increasing number show growing sensitivity to related ethical questions.

In 16 years in state government in Illinois I have seen a marked improvement in the reduction of corruption. We now have a committee to police potential abuses in this area, as do both houses of congress. But having said that, it nevertheless is true that problems remain. Some public officials still are willing to abuse a public trust.

What can be done about them?

There is no substitute for an alert electorate, people who pay close attention to the officials they elect.

In addition to that, there is a relatively simple safeguard which would help restore public confidence and place a barrier in the way of any public official who might be tempted to abuses.

That safeguard is public disclosure of income in detail. It not only would make clear the sources of revenue, but it also would protect the official who must make decisions in areas where he may have a financial conflict of interest. Certain conflicts of interest are inevitable, and the evil is not with the conflict as much as with the fact that the public sometimes does not know of the conflict and cannot make a judgment. For instance, a farmer in the legislature should not abstain from voting on farm legislation, or voicing his opinion on it, yet this is an obvious conflict of interest. An insurance executive should not refrain from using his knowledge of insurance problems to help his legislative colleagues. But this should be out in the open, so the public can decide whether an official is serving his own interests or the public's.

Following the example of Senator Paul Douglas, a former public servant I admire greatly, I have made public in detail my income during each of the 16 years I have held public office. Now, as lieutenant governor, I require income disclosure from my administrative assistants.

There are advantages in this for the public servant. To a great extent, it removes the question of possible improper motivation. People may disagree with a decision you make, or question an opinion you express, but if to that is added the suspicion that you are filling your own pocketbook, your action or opinion takes on a totally different cast. To the extent that we can remove the question of financial motivation from politics, we will increase the chance for healthy discussion, free of distrust.

The disadvantages to public disclosure of income are few. Your neighbors will learn how much you make, but they probably have a good idea, anyway. People may question the wisdom of your investments—and you probably join them in that.

It is important that disclosure should be *in detail*, not just a reporting of your income tax statement. My detailed income disclosure for 1970, for example, shows a gross income of $42,949.46 for my wife and myself, plus about $20 for each for my children. (It should be added here that the expenses of a public official are greater than those of most citizens.) Our income includes my state salary of $28,896.71; $1,137.71 from book royalties; dividends on my limited stock holdings varying from $259.95 on National Aviation to 12 cents from one share of Brunswick; travel expense reimbursements, and honorariums from colleges, universities, and a variety of groups, all spelled out precisely. That is sent to every newspaper and radio station in the state and is available for anyone who wants it. My statement also notes that we own our home, but have a mortgage of $14,292.15 on it; that I owe the Troy Security Bank $5,700, and I owe my stockbroker $1,538.98. The eight-page mimeographed document spells out my financial situation in gruesome detail.

Perhaps as important as the disclosure itself is the public reaction to it. Sometimes people come up to me on the street and say, "You're the only politician who can do that!" That is not true, of course, but the comment itself reveals public attitudes. There is no question that the public appreciates this and, happily, the practice is spreading in Illinois on a voluntary basis. Soon I hope we can go beyond the voluntary basis and require it, at least from key elected and appointed officials. Because of the difficulties the judiciary has experienced in Illinois, I have suggested that in our state the judiciary would be a good place to start. If this were required of the judiciary, my guess is that it would spread to the other branches of government.

With few exceptions, meetings of public bodies ought to open to the public.

Public business should be exactly that; yet an amazing number of officials for some reason believe that once elected to office they have a right to do business behind closed doors, excluding their bosses, the citizens. In Illinois we now have a law making such a practice illegal except for a few rare instances, such as when a real estate purchase is being considered, or when information is being discussed about personnel to be hired or fired.

In most states, public bodies—from the legislature on down—still conduct meetings in secret. It is a reprehensible practice, even though those doing it may be most sincere. Their excuses are familiar: "We can speak more frankly if the press and public are not present." Or: "We're free from pressure this way."

There are two major defects with such proceedings:

1. While the secret meeting may not be abused by most public officials, it is a shield for the corrupt. Those who abuse public office should not have such a shield.

2. Secret meetings go against the spirit of a free system, for the theory of our government is not only that citizens have a right to know what decisions are reached, but that they also have an equally important right to know *how* decisions are reached. If they have not had a chance to hear all the arguments on a specific issue, it may be difficult

to understand how a decision was reached. The public body protects itself when it throws its doors open and lets it be known that anyone may enter.

Secrecy not only is abused at the state and local level, but also in congress. Despite recent improvements, far too many committee meetings are secret when they should not be. "Security" frequently is given as a reason; sometimes this is valid, though often it is not. Security is used too often as an excuse for denying access to both records and meetings. A few years ago the freedom of information committee of Sigma Delta Chi, the professional journalism fraternity, disclosed that when one newspaper tried to find out how much peanut butter the army bought, it was denied the information for reasons of security because, as they explained, if you know how much peanut butter is purchased you can figure out the number of men in the army. Down the hall in another Pentagon office they were handing out the actual figures of how many men were in the army!

That is an extreme example but there are too many such examples at all levels of government where records are unnecessarily kept secret, and where meetings are, too.

Legislative bodies, city councils, school boards (the worst abusers of secrecy, though this has improved), health district boards, library boards and all others should be open to citizens. If you are in a community or state where meetings are not open to the public, then you are in a community or state where change is needed.

More direct involvement by the public in the processes of government must be encouraged.

This can include such basic things as citizen advisory groups to park districts or to mental health programs. Mayors, governors and other officials frequently could use citizen advisory groups to good advantage, though they should be genuinely consulted and not used as a cover-up, as too often is the case. What sometimes happens is that a government agency—on projects ranging from highways to housing—makes a decision and *then* hearings are held by those who already have made the decision; or a citizens' advisory committee is appointed, but the agency involved knows that this is just frosting on the cake and it goes ahead with its plans, paying no attention to the advisory group. These things discourage citizen participation.

One of the most important areas for advisory groups right now is in police-community relations, particularly in large cities and in campus communities. Such committees can be most helpful to the community and to the police.

Beyond this type of citizen participation, the process should be opened up more. Here are two examples:

In the early days of the state of Illinois, one of the legislative committees was the committee on petitions. Any petition by a group of citizens automatically went to this committee for consideration. It meant direct access by citizens to the legislature on any matter which concerned them. It is true that at the present time people may write to legislators and almost all legislators read their mail and consider matters presented there. But to have direct consideration by a committee and to have the opportunity to testify before a committee in behalf of a petition took the process one step further. It gave people a chance to learn more directly how government works, and it also gave them an opportunity to explain their views in some depth to several legislators. Along the way this system was discarded by Illinois, but I believe there is much to recommend it for many governmental bodies. In smaller governmental units, a citizen ordinarily can meet directly with officials on a problem or proposal.

A unique approach is offered by Massachusetts. Any citizen there can file a bill (measure) for consideration and it is automatically referred to the appropriate committee. It means more work for the Massachusetts legislature; more bills are introduced there than in any other state. But it gives people direct access to the law-making process that they do not have in any other state. After the proposal from a citizen is assigned to a committee, he is notified when a public hearing will be held. He may testify at that hearing, along with other witnesses he may wish to bring. Those who wish to testify against the measure also are heard. One high-ranking Massachusetts official summed it up: "It means more work for us, but it fits into the New England tradition of having the people directly involved in the decision-making process."

Other approaches have been tried, such as giving citizens the right to place a matter on a ballot through petition; but new approaches are needed.

I like the early Illinois approach, and that of Massachusetts, because it reduces the distance between a citizen and his government. The feeling of remoteness from government is particularly acute in urban areas, and increasingly we are becoming an urban society. Recently I was a "Politician in Residence" for one week at Hunter College in New York City. Members of one class I met were working on advance degrees. They were people who had important insights into the needs of citizens and what government must do, but their deep-seated distrust and attitude of hopelessness toward government startled me, and they had extremely limited insights into what *they* actually could do. Of course, if people become too negative, too cynical, they will accomplish nothing because they will attempt nothing.

That sense of hopelessness, I find, grows with the size of

a community. In New York the feeling is more intense than in Chicago; in Chicago it is more intense than in Peoria; in Peoria, more intense than in Coal City. The need for creating avenues of approach to government is particularly important in states with major cities. There the problems are more intense, and there the people should have a feeling that *their* government will listen and help.

Many believe that the system of electing a president should relate more directly to the will of the majority of voters.

Some of you will disagree that change is desirable, though I am among those who would like to see some responsible change. It violates something that I sense is fundamental in the selection process when one candidate receives a majority of the popular vote but his opponent receives a majority of the electoral vote and is declared the winner.

The problem of who should vote and for what office always has been a matter of controversy. During the new nation's Constitutional Convention, George Mason, who eventually played a major role in drafting the Bill of Rights, held a debate with James Madison. Madison argued for a direct election while Mason said that he would as soon trust the selection of colors to a blind man as the selection of the president to the people. Fortunately, Mason's view did not prevail.

For some years, ownership of property was necessary to be eligible to vote in many states. Thomas Paine commented: "You require that a man shall have 60 dollars worth of property or he shall not vote. Here is a man today who owns a jackass, and the jackass is worth 60 dollars. Today the man is a voter, and he goes to the polls with his jackass and deposits his vote. Tomorrow his jackass dies. The man then goes to vote without his jackass and he cannot vote at all. Now tell me, which was the voter? The man or the jackass?"

Our system of selecting public officials has evolved gradually, but not without its defects. Many believe that the system of presidential selection which permits the will of the majority to be voided is one of those defects. Any change, however, must be carefully worked out, because the two-party system may not always be with us. It is based primarily on tradition. I am among those who believe that we are fortunate to have such a tradition. However, if in the years ahead we move toward a multiparty system, we may not always have a clear-cut choice. For that reason I do not favor totally discarding the electoral college system. But I believe that a system that would give the nation stability in the event of the growth of more parties, yet permits the will of the nation's majority to be decisive, merits adoption.

2.

Religion and Politics: Match or Mismatch?

You can skip this chapter, but I hope you won't because I want to explore the question of motivation and the relationship of the religious faith to problems of life which young people face.

I don't want to turn you off if you feel no particular church allegiance right now, or if you are hostile to organized religion as you see it. Abraham Lincoln, for example, was in a sense deeply religious, but he had no church affiliation—and no one would question his significant contributions.

What does religion have to do with politics?

Plenty—if you and I mean the same by "religion."

By "religion" I don't mean the routine you and I may have established of going to church on Sunday. For me—and perhaps for you—that is sometimes more habit than anything else. Certainly, by itself it is not a sure indication of faith.

32

I am bold enough to call myself a Christian, though I feel I live my faith most inadequately. But it troubles me even to refer to myself as a Christian because too often this seems to express an "I am better than you are" attitude. I don't mean to imply that, either with my profession of faith or my church affiliation, which happens to be Lutheran. Also, by "religion" I do not mean an emotional attachment to an organization. For some I sense that the attachment to a church or a faith has about as much to do with the realities of life and faith as does an attachment to a high school football team. They are happy when "our team" wins one; there are cheers at the appropriate time, and they think the clergy are not supposed to be anything more than cheerleaders. (If the "cheerleaders" say anything more than "Fight, team fight," or "Our team is all right," some people in the bleachers get all shook up.)

Anyone who has ever thought more than casually about the meaning of life and death has some kind of theology. It may be imprecise; it may be a feeling which is never expressed to anyone, or it may be expressed in terms which are anything but "theological."

When a Communist speaks of "the great unknown" (a phrase which sounds much like some early American Indian religious expressions), he is expressing a form of theology —though he would deny it vigorously. Carl Sandburg, who would lay no claim to being a theologian, wrote, "Something began me and it had no beginning: something will end me and it has no end."

Recognition of God ranges from those who admit a simple awareness of a great mystery about life, to those who claim to know with great precision all of the ultimate realities. Recently I took part in a program inaugurating the second annual "Olympics for the Retarded." The Joseph P.

Kennedy Foundation for the Retarded supported the program financially, and I was seated on the platform next to Mrs. R. Sargent Shriver, the former Eunice Kennedy, sister of John F. Kennedy and Robert Kennedy. One speaker said, "Let us not forget that smiling down upon us on this occasion are three people who applaud what you are doing, Joseph P. Kennedy, John F. Kennedy, and Robert Kennedy." It was an emotional touch to the opening ceremonies and I did not know how Eunice might be reacting. She leaned over and whispered to me, "He has much more detailed information about the hereafter than I do."

I find myself somewhere between those who speak only in vague generalities and those who know everything with great certainty and in great detail.

Perhaps if I had more time to read and reflect I would join those who are precise and certain about everything, though I doubt it. I accept the fact that I cannot come close to ultimate truths entirely through reason, that somewhere there must occur what Kierkegaard calls "the leap of faith." Though I realize I cannot separate my personal background from my present position, speaking from that position of faith, I generally do not find it uncomfortable or illogical.

I read what I can—the basic Christian documents and the writings of people like Dietrich Bonnhoefer and Rabbi Abraham Heschel who has valid insights and who speaks for many of us when he writes: "Little does contemporary religion ask of man. It is ready to offer comfort; it has no courage to challenge. It is ready to offer edification; it has no courage to break the idols, to shatter callousness. The trouble is that religion has become 'religion'—institution, dogma, ritual. . . . When faith is completely replaced by creed, worship by discipline, love by habit; when the crisis of today is ignored because of the splendor of the past; when faith becomes an heirloom rather than a living fountain; when religion speaks only in the name of authority rather than with the voice of compassion, its message becomes meaningless." *

Important for me is the personal determination that I am not destined to be a great theologian, nor even a poor one. While I must continue to search for truth and new insights, I have the responsibility to act on the insights I have now. My call in life is not to draw up new theological theses, but to live—however inadequately—the faith which I profess.

I remember what a chaplain at an Indian reservation once told me: "I don't worry about serving Christ. I serve my fellow human being and then I know I am serving Christ." At the time I thought it was poor theology, but when you read Matthew 25, you see that Christ also said that.

This is what the story of the Good Samaritan (who more accurately should have been called the Hated Samaritan) tells us. The message which comes through the Old Testament again and again is that of service to your fellow human being. Read Amos, or portions of Isaiah, and it is clear that what these prophets want is not people who respect pious words, but those who are willing to help the poor and oppressed.

The Christian faith is a *doing* faith.

During a campaign I occasionally meet people who tell me, "You're a Lutheran and I'm a Lutheran, too. I'm going to vote for you." I always have an uncomfortable feeling because, candidly, I don't like to turn down votes, but if I

---

* Quoted in *The Promise of Heschel*, by Franklin Sherman. Philadelphia: J. P. Lippincott, 1970, p. 85.

have a chance to explain, I try to point out that if my opponent is a Presbyterian, or a Catholic, or an Anglican, or a Jew, and he is a better man for the job than I am, then my Lutheran friends have the obligation to support him and not me.

Fortunately, prejudicial voting because of religion is diminishing. A 1937 Gallup Poll showed that 46 per cent of the voting population would not vote for a candidate for president if he was Jewish. By 1969 the same poll showed that only 8 per cent of the population still held the same views—still too high but a substantial improvement. In 1964 Senator Barry Goldwater, whose father was Jewish, though the senator was not raised in the Jewish faith, became the Republican presidential candidate. No one in either political party thought his defeat was caused by his Jewish background—though the Goldwater candidacy moved Jewish writer Harry Golden to note: "I always knew the first Jewish president would be an Episcopalian."

A more subtle temptation is for people active in church affairs to equate their position on a particular measure as the Christian position. Sometimes I agree with the position they take, and sometimes I disagree. I find that the difficulty in disagreeing is that people like this put you in the position of seeming to argue with God, and that's a bit rough!

I hope no one assumes that I have a special pipeline to the Almighty so that I know precisely what should be done. But a distinction must be made between a concern for those who take seriously the command to love their neighbor, and the method for expressing that concern. For example, all of us who care about others and who think seriously about what they believe must be concerned about hunger on the face of the earth. But *how* we show that concern is not precisely spelled out in any religion documents we consider inspired.

What I most fear, however, is not the sincere but naive person who makes judgments which may not be too sound; I fear more the person who thinks he is faithful to his church or creed, but who remains comfortably aloof and indifferent to the problems of human beings around him. I think that he is, in fact, betraying his faith. This is the clear lesson from Germany. With few exceptions, Protestants and Catholics were silent when Hitler began to persecute the Jews. Even some religious journals in the United States were amazingly silent, and silence was all that tyranny needed.

Happily, I see no Adolph Hitlers on the immediate horizon, but there are other tyrannies which we defend when we are silent. The same country which produced Hitler also produced Martin Luther, a religious leader who had his strengths and weaknesses. Once he wrote: "So this is now the mark by which we all shall certainly know whether the birth of the Lord Christ is effective in us: If we take upon ourselves the need of our neighbor."

The political arena is a major place for doing that.

3.

Why Not Turn People On, Not Off?

Recently Illinois completed work for a new state constitution. One of the questions the constitutional convention tackled concerned whether or not 18-year-olds should vote.

Several groups around the state formed to promote the idea, and four officers of one group came to our office for an opinion on how they should proceed, since I had long advocated voting for 18-year-olds. They explained their plans, including an idea for a dramatic camp-out on the lawns of all convention delegates who would not commit themselves to supporting the vote for 18-year-olds. Further, they planned to continue their camp-out until the delegates would agree to extending the franchise to 18-year-olds.

I told them that if they were interested in headlines, their plan was excellent. They could expect radio, TV, and newspaper coverage. But if their aim was to get something passed at the convention, their strategy would backfire. They would lose votes rather than gain them. I suggested that if they wanted to gain votes, it would be much wiser for them to volunteer to mow lawns, rather than camp on them!

This is an isolated example of one strange phenomenon of today: the belief that if you do something dramatic that makes news, you are automatically helping your cause. In reality, you may be ruining any chance for success.

We are seeing this experience repeated in the fields of human relations, in religion, in education, in virtually every area where there is controversy—and there are few areas where there is no controversy these days.

I sense that in some cases there really is less interest in the cause people say they want to support than there is in a desire to satisfy a deep-seated emotional need for attention. If you can't get it through normal behavior, you do the abnormal, and that gets attention. So much of the abnormal behavior which arouses public anger more properly should arouse sympathy. That does not excuse behavior which is either in terribly poor taste or causes violence, but it explains part of it. (While I do not agree with it entirely, an excellent article on this subject has been reprinted from *Encounter* magazine in pamphlet form—*Obsolete Youth*, by Bruno Bettelheim, published by San Francisco Press, 225 12th Street, San Francisco, California. It sells for 50 cents.)

The need for recognition is regarded by psychologists as a basic emotional need for every human being. That is why in certain periods of life which often are accompanied by emotional stress—such as adolescence—the need for attention is more pronounced; there is, for example, a tendency to dress differently. Many of those who are critical of you now looked a bit strange when they were your age. When I was in high school, it was the fad to wear dirty cords (corduroy pants); when our outraged parents had them washed, we immediately marked them thoroughly with pencils, crayons and everything else to be in style. Saddle shoes were popular, but, again, they had to be filthy. And fellows wore atrocious-looking things called "zoot suits," which I shall not bore you by describing. Young people have always had a tendency to be different during their years of growing toward maturity. Some mature more rapidly than others; some never do.

The emotionally immature have a greater need for recognition, and sometimes this is carried over into politics in an unhealthy way. There are healthy ways of getting recognition, and unhealthy. The latter may satisfy some inner struggles, but they can do great damage to society as a whole. Psychological victories may produce political setbacks.

I do not mean to suggest that young people actively interested in causes are sick. Among the activists, only a small minority resort to extremes in behavior. Within that small minority there probably is a high percentage who have serious emotional problems; there also are those who are basically healthy, but whose sense of idealism has been exploited or misdirected.

A troubled emotional life easily leads to a deep-seated bitterness which I have seen occasionally. It is frightening, for it will not diminish a person's emotional problems; it will multiply them. Disappointment is part of the lot of man; bitterness is not necessarily his lot. Long before this troubled era, Tennyson wrote:

> "Ah, what shall I be at fifty,
> Should nature keep me alive,
> If I find the world so bitter,
> When I am but twenty-five?"

Bitterness is like quick-sand, easy to enter but difficult to escape, once you have been trapped. Bitterness is sometimes both the cause and the consequence of extreme conduct. By extreme conduct I mean the use of dynamite to blast buildings and stones to break windows; the unwillingness, by chanting and shouting, to let someone speak or to allow others to hear him; the constant use of four-letter words. I do *not* mean the wearing of long hair, although unfortunately it is true that because of the conduct of a few there is strong public feeling against young men with long hair. (It may mean that if an "all-American" image wins converts, you will have to choose between your present habits and political effectiveness.)

The public also tends to confuse the "hippie," who is a drop-out from society, with the student political activist who frequently dresses like a hippie. A paper written by two University of Denver scholars points out that while hippies strongly reject the ideals of their parents, student activists actually are accepting the views of their parents and following through on them. While generally praising student activists, they note:

"Although activists were found to be able in academic pursuits, they could also be characterized as simplistic. . . . .The premises, values and beliefs which he [the activist] accepted were regarded as in the nature of absolutes, it being implied that persons who deviate with respect to these are either stupid, ignorant, dishonest or weak: in particular, those of the Establishment who thus deviate were so regarded.

"It should be recognized, however, that simplistic thinking is not uncommon among youths generally, activist or not. . . . It is not unusual for a youth to become entranced with some kind of ideology or grand design that supposedly explains the cause of all evil and injustice. The limitations of the ideology are disregarded or denied in a cavalier fashion. Later, as the everyday battles and demands of life force the realization of limitations upon the young adult, he begins to modify his 'absolutes.' At this time he becomes 'compromised' in the eyes of his younger colleagues. . . . Not everyone 'outgrows' this state; there are adults who proceed through life without ever questioning the 'absolutes' of their world views." *

"But," you ask, "whether you call views simplistic or absolute, isn't it basically true in our society today that crime pays? Are not the dramatic confrontations which violate the law the most effective way of moving ahead in our society?"

Let's examine this contention.

Depending on the local laws and ordinances, it may not be a crime to shout and jeer and chant, and thus not permit someone to speak. If a national figure is involved, you may make NBC, ABC, or CBS television news. And what have you done? Here are two practical examples. When George Wallace started campaigning for the presidency, I saw the television news spots where people heckled him and a few times stopped him from speaking. That was a campaign year for me, and as I moved around our state I quickly sensed the tide of Wallace votes rising. The hecklers were making votes for Wallace! I supported Hubert Humphrey in his race against Richard Nixon and George Wallace, and I know my own reaction when a small group of hecklers in

* John L. Horn and Paul D. Knott of the University of Denver. Unpublished paper, "Activist Youth of the 1960's: A Profile and Prognosis."

Rockford, Illinois, were rude to Humphrey. Perhaps 30 people began chanting and trying to interrupt things. But there were 15,000 to 20,000 present that afternoon, and those 30 ended up producing sympathy, enthusiasm, and votes for Humphrey.

Much more important than how this conduct alters votes is that it violates something that is basic in our system of government and essential to the preservation of freedom. The most fundamental premise of our system is that all of us have a right to speak freely—no matter how much we may disagree with others' viewpoints—and that those with the soundest ideas ultimately will prevail. Those who discourage a free flow of ideas weaken the nation and imperil freedom.

What has violence on the campus accomplished?

First, we must realize that violence is rare, despite the headlines. There is a sense of idealism and concern among high school and college students today that did not exist a decade ago. While there are occasional excesses, something fundamentally good has happened.

In Illinois—and I can best judge only in Illinois—the two colleges which have made the most headway in giving students a real voice in campus programs have had virtually no violence.

Violence has had one dramatic effect: It has changed the political climate from one in which challenging a university budget request meant political disaster for a legislator, to one in which such a challenge means votes. The budget requests of the governor of Illinois clearly reflect this. The 1970 budget request (made in April, 1969) for our two big state universities, the University of Illinois and Southern Illinois University, showed a large increase. The University of Illinois had a 10.8 per cent increase and

Southern Illinois University an increase of 33.2 per cent. By April, 1970, while the state budget generally showed an increase of approximately 15 per cent, the budget request for the University of Illinois was increased only 1.2 per cent and Southern Illinois University's budget was cut by 1.6 per cent. Violence by a handful of students produced an anti-higher education political climate, and hurt the universities in more than the immediately obvious ways. Students who throw stones, break windows, and take over administration buildings ultimately are depriving others of a chance for an education.

In addition, violence on a campus goes against all the best traditions. If there is one place in a state or nation where mind and not muscle should prevail, it is on the college campus.

The political arena is another place where reason should prevail. It does not always. But the cause you are pushing is much more likely to be considered by the public if it is presented without violence and in good taste.

You ask: "Hasn't violence brought financial support to street gangs? Hasn't violence paid off for the Ku Klux Klan? Hasn't it paid off for the Black Panthers? Doesn't the nation's black population have to resort to violence in order to achieve progress?"

Unfortunately it is true that in some areas social conditions have been allowed to deteriorate to the point where violence became almost inevitable, and when that violence occurred, attention focused on the area and temporary improvements were the result. But along with the violence—and sometimes the improvements—have come some emotional tensions and deepening divisions in the community at large which have not been healthy.

The violence of the Civil War ended slavery, but if we

had had the good sense to abolish slavery without war, millions of lives would have been saved, some of the deepseated animosities which still exist would no longer be present, and many of the racial tensions of today would not exist, either, for progress would have been more rapid.

That is easy to see from the perspective of more than a century. Unfortunately it is easier to make accurate historical judgments than accurate appraisals of the current scene. However, two conclusions can safely be drawn:

1. In almost all cases, violence could have been avoided had we paid more attention to an area's immediate social problems. In most instances violence was not planned, but had some reasonably sophisticated efforts been made to resolve certain problems, they would have been reduced in scope, and the likelihood of violence also would have been diminished.

2. While violence may produce some immediate results, there is a good possibility that the lessons of history will apply to our era, and that temporary gains will be more than offset by long-range losses. When John Wilkes Booth killed Lincoln he thought he was helping the South; the result was tragic for the South and for the nation. In 1837, when a mob killed the Abolitionist editor, Elijah Lovejoy, because of his anti-slavery writings, it snuffed out the life of one man—but gave the anti-slavery movement its greatest boost until the publication of *Uncle Tom's Cabin.* No group did more to pass the sweeping Civil Rights Act of 1964 than the Ku Klux Klan, because their violence shocked the conscience of the nation. How much harm the Black Panthers have done to the cause of human relations is not so easily calculated, but no one who is reasonably sensitive can doubt the damage.

Mayor John Lindsay of New York recently said this in a speech at the University of California at Berkeley: "There are those who will tell you that violence and terror is [sic] a tactical mistake. It is. But it is something far, far more than that. It is cowardly and it is immoral. It wrecks havoc among innocents, whether they be workers in an office building, or peasants in a Vietnamese village. And if you claim to believe the Vietnam war is immoral—if you understand why the burning of a village and the slaughter of civilians is an abhorrent act—then your job and my job is not to open a new frontier for bloodshed, but to stop it everywhere, once and for all."

A friend notes, "The American Indian has done almost nothing to draw attention to his plight and he has the lowest life expectancy and the highest infant mortality rate of any ethnic group in the United States. If violence is not necessary, why is nothing done for the Indian?"

In fact, the American Indian has tried two courses, both unsuccessful. The first was the violence of the Indian wars of the nineteenth century and it produced only more violence. The second has been equally disastrous: quiet acceptance of oppression. The answer for the American Indian, as well as for other groups, is neither silence nor violence, but reasonable appeals to the conscience of the nation. We need to hear a cry for help.

There is an understandable attraction to the problems of blacks and others: "We are being abused. Violence is the only answer. Let's revolt and stop this." This simplistic but emotionally satisfying answer contains some dangers.

First, while the person who says that probably will not try violence when he begins to mature and examine the realities, there are others who are not as well equipped to examine realities. They may take seriously the advocate of violence, ultimately causing violence, retarding progress, and perhaps ruining their lives, if not ending them.

Second, the call for revolution becomes a synthetic substitute for genuinely doing something to achieve progress; it channels energy into what can most charitably be called nonproductive areas.

Third, that kind of talk turns off many people in our society who could help greatly and who could be turned on with the right kind of appeal.

Perhaps that is a good summation of what I have been trying to say here: Turn people on, not off.

THEN HOW CAN YOU BE EFFECTIVE?

Following the entrance of United States troops into Cambodia in the spring of 1970, many student leaders throughout the country felt that something should be done to demonstrate their opposition to this move, and to try to change public opinion. They knew that a sizable body of public opinion held back from associating with the antiwar cause because so many people had opposed the war in ways the public found distasteful.

Sam Brown, the chief organizer of the Vietnam Moratorium, recently was quoted by the *New York Times* as saying, "The potential peace voters in Middle America don't like long hair, campus protests, or, in short, anything which irritates the nerve endings of middle-class values. They may dislike the war, but they dislike radicals far more. The outline of a successful anti-war strategy, it seems to me, is clear: the appeal must be made in such a way that middle Americans will not ignore the substance of the argument because of an offensive style."

Student leaders, sensing the accuracy of that statement, started becoming more sophisticated in their appeals. Students who dressed neatly and conventionally were sent to Rotary Clubs to speak, to Chamber of Commerce dinners, to coffee hours in homes. They passed petitions and politely asked people to sign them. In short, students not only helped to mold public opinion, but they also learned how to be effective. They learned the complexities of slowly but steadily adding supporters to a cause.

Any successful effort in behalf of a cause or a candidate involves building coalitions, and attracting people rather than repelling them.

When I served as a legislator I was fortunate to see many bills which I sponsored, passed but few of them passed without some type of coalition of interests. If I had waited to get a majority only from those who agreed with me on all aspects of a measure, nothing ever would have passed. You point out the advantage a proposal would have to one region, then the advantage (which might be totally different) to another area.

Here is a practical example: I was the chief sponsor of a measure declaring it public policy in Illinois that meetings of boards, commissions, committees, and others receiving tax money should be open to the public. The first session I introduced the bill, I lost it in committee. Two years later I tried again. I went to the various groups which either had not supported it or had opposed it, and in my second try I was able to get their support. Surprisingly, many newspapers had not supported it at first, but in my second try I was able to get their support. The first time around, the Chicago City Council opposed it: I pointed out to them that since their meetings already were open, they had nothing to lose by supporting the measure, and it actually would put them in a favorable light. The worst offenders on closed meetings had been the school boards, and the executive secretary of the Illinois School Board Association readily agreed that their closed meetings had created bad public relations. He testified for the bill. Gradually I built up support from a variety of groups which favored the measure and it passed. If you can build a big enough coalition, a bill will pass.

Whether it is the war in Vietnam or open meetings, whether you are supporting a candidate for the school board or a candidate for the presidency of the United States, you must convince people that it is in their own best interest to support your cause or your candidate.

Let's say that you live in a community which badly needs a swimming pool. One approach would be to get 20 of your friends lined up to stop all traffic on the main street. But a much wiser course would be to get those friends together to talk about how you can enlist the help of the Lions Club, the Women's Club, and other groups, and then have someone from your group speak to them. Get the 20 to make a list of the 100 most influential persons in your community and plan a strategy for getting each one of those 100 in your corner. Some have children who would enjoy swimming, and arousing the interest of these parents should not be difficult. Perhaps two people have service stations; you could point out to them that a swimming pool would keep at home some of the local business that now goes out of town, as well as bringing additional business to the community. A restaurant owner could be enlisted for the same reasons. The police chief should be interested because a pool would give young people recreation and help keep them off the streets. Keep on going down the list, and plan carefully. Soon you will have found a way to line up at least 90 of those 100 on your side. It is not as quick and dramatic as stopping traffic in the street, but infinitely more effective.

You will have built a coalition of interests, and this is essential to any action in politics, whether it is a swimming pool for a community of 3,000; consideration for a program for Puerto Ricans in a community of three million, or trying to guide a major new bill through congress.

A coalition also is essential in electing a candidate, even a candidate who seems to be primarily a one-issue candidate. In 1968, the number of votes for George Wallace were not due entirely to the racial issue; he also had some "little guy fighting the big bully" support for his stand on economic issues.

During the first part of the 1968 campaign, Senator Eugene McCarthy was viewed almost entirely as an anti-Vietnam candidate. After the Wisconsin primary, in which he defeated President Johnson, the widespread belief was that this was a tremendous slap at the President's foreign policy. That assertion contained some truth. But on the same day as the primary, Madison, Wisconsin, had a city referendum on a cease fire and withdrawal of United States troops from Vietnam. The vote was 58 per cent to 42 per cent in opposition to the proposal and in support of the President's position. The "yes" vote carried only 10 of the city's 41 precincts. But McCarthy carried all 41 precincts in the city. Obviously, even in this supposedly clear-cut election, there had been a coalition of interests which supported McCarthy. The vote did not center solely on the war issue. After the New Hampshire primary, which preceded that in Wisconsin, a poll taken by the University of Michigan Survey Research Center showed that three out of five of those who voted for McCarthy strongly disagreed with him on Vietnam.

After President Johnson's withdrawal from the 1968 presidential race, the contest in the primaries centered around Senator McCarthy and Senator Robert Kennedy. The best illustration of the need for a candidate to build a coalition of interests is shown by the following list of committees formed by Kennedy supporters to promote his campaign:

Academic
Architects and Engineers
Arts
Businessmen
Clergy
Communications
Editors and Publishers
Entertainment
Ex-Peace Corps and Ex-Vista
Farmers
Former Public Officials
Indians
Labor and Civil Service
Law Enforcement Officials
Nationalities (a number of groups here)
Negroes
Philanthropists
Physicians
Republicans
Scientists and Engineers
Senior Citizens
Social Workers

Spanish-Speaking
Sports
State and Local Public Officials
Students
Teachers
Veterans
Women's Groups *

In some states there were additional committees.

In 1966 Robert Kennedy said, "In such a fantastic and dangerous world we will not find answers in old dogmas, by repeating outworn slogans, or fighting on ancient battlegrounds against fading enemies long after the real struggle has moved on. We ourselves must change to master change. We must rethink our old ideas and beliefs before they capture and destroy us. And for those answers America must look to its young people, the children of this time of change. And we look especially to that privileged minority of educated men who are the students of America."

Kennedy meant every word of that appeal, which he addressed to students. But if you will check the record, you also will find that he made appeals to postal workers, to the police, to those of Polish background, to senior citizens, to businessmen, and to many others who make up the nation's fabric.

No appeal is less sincere than another, because all elements are needed to build a better society. Any serious candidate has to build in a variety of ways, just as everyone

* Quoted in *The Real Majority*, by Richard Scammon and Ben J. Wattenberg. New York: Coward-McCann, p. 77

who wishes to be effective within the political system must do so, also.

Here are three practical areas where you can test your ability to be effective:

1. Take a look at your community and find some relatively small project that needs doing. It may be removing a dead tree, or there may be an empty house that should be torn down. Perhaps you have no library services, or the service available needs improvement. Maybe the garbage service should be improved. Maybe a stream is badly polluted or an industry pollutes the air. Perhaps junked cars are an eye-sore. I don't care where you live, if you will sit down and start analyzing your community, you can come up with at least 20 minor projects which need doing. Then find out how you can get action within your community.

The late football coach, Vince Lombardi, said shortly before his death: "What this country needs is fewer flag wavers and fewer flag burners, and more people who will look at problems and come up with sensible answers." That's what I am asking you to do here: Look at a problem and try to come up with a sensible answer. As important as the results from the project itself will be the fact that you will learn how government actually works—not as you read about it, but as you can experience it.

2. Look for a political candidate to support. You don't need to be 18 or 21 to do effective political work. Most political candidates would welcome your volunteer efforts. You won't be writing speeches or making policy decisions, but you will be doing the essential work of passing out literature or stuffing envelopes—or any one of a thousand

other tasks which are essential in a good campaign. Take a hard look at the candidates who present themselves in the next election. Find one you believe in. Don't expect to agree with him 100 per cent; you don't always agree with your parents or your boyfriend or girlfriend, either. Be mature enough to evaluate the candidate on a number of factors, not just one. In picking a candidate, don't look just at the more highly publicized races for president, senator or governor, but look, also, at the races for congress, for the state legislature, for county offices. When you have your candidate picked out, write to him or go to his office and tell him that you are interested in helping. You will find that you not only help the candidate, but help yourself by learning in a down-to-earth way how politics works.

3. Take an interest in one of the bigger issues mentioned in the next chapters. In most of these areas you will find progress painfully slow, and it will be more difficult to measure the success of your efforts. But all of these larger issues relate in one way or another to the problems of your own community, though that relationship may not be obvious. Once you pick an area, join with others who have similar interests. It may be a Mental Health Association, a group to help retarded children, a United Nations association, a civil rights organization, a group fighting pollution, a conservation club. There is no shortage of organizations and causes. Again, not only will you be doing some good, but you will be helping yourself learn how to change government policy.

A fourth suggestion should be mentioned, though I sense it is one that may not interest many young people: Get involved in a political party. You probably do not yet identify readily with either political party; yet many of the most crucial decisions will be made by party leaders. It would be helpful to be active enough to at least learn how the political structure in your area works. The local leader of your party probably would welcome your volunteer efforts.

One added note which is good advice, whether you decide to help in the political arena, or never do: Be friendly, not only to those who agree with you but also to those who disagree. If you are friendly, it takes some of the sting and bitterness from whatever an opponent may say. When we talk about political participation, we are speaking of areas of great controversy. Your attitude will help determine whether the controversy is held at a high plane of discussion or degenerates into something personal and bitter.

Pope John XXIII once said: "I don't care what they say or think of me. I must be good and kind always to everybody."

Pope John would have made a good politician.

4.

What Are Some of the Basic Issues?

A few areas where change in the process is needed already have been discussed. Now I will cover some of the broader issues. Each section will end with some specific suggestions as to what you might do. I have had to omit some areas for the sake of brevity. Writing concisely about complex issues results in some oversimplification, for which I apologize. Without exception, every topic mentioned has some relationship to all of the others, whether it has to do with international or national problems.

DISARMAMENT

Today the United States and the Soviet Union each have enough nuclear weapons to destroy every city on the face of the earth with a population of more than 50,000. Three other nations have the knowledge to do the same: mainland China, France and Great Britain. Nineteen other nations are developing nuclear capability.

Will these stockpiles of weapons be used? Up to this point in history, there have been few major stockpiles of any type of weapon that have not been used. The lesson of history suggests that the question should be: Is it possible that these stockpiles of weapons will not be used?

In addition to the horror of the millions of people who would be killed, the building of bigger and bigger and more and more effective arms systems costs the nations of the world hundreds of billions of dollars which could be used instead to lift the lot of man. The United States' defense budget is between 50 per cent and 73 per cent of our total national budget, depending on how the figures are calculated. If half of that amount were to be used to help the underprivileged within our own country and the other half for those beyond our borders, both the nation and the world would be an unbelievably better place in which to live.

Costa Rica's constitution prohibits armed forces, and this frees policy-makers to use their funds for other purposes. I asked the president of Costa Rica whether he would recommend this if he were a United States leader, and he replied, "No. Absolutely not. I hope the day will come when you can, but certainly world stability would be threatened if you were to abandon all arms now."

Unfortunately he is correct. Until there are other means of protecting ourselves and the smaller nations of the world, it is essential for the major powers—and most smaller powers—to continue to have an armed force. It is our insurance against attack from beyond our borders.

One difficulty with this "insurance" is that it is explosive —it could be detonated, if we are not careful. The other problem is much like that of people who buy so much insurance that they are insurance-poor.

What can be done?

1. The United Nations must be strengthened so that it can become the policing agency for the nations. If this can be done, arms reduction could follow.

2. We can encourage agreements between nations. As this is being typed, the United States and the Soviet Union are in serious negotiation on arms limitation, the SALT (Strategic Arms Limitation Talks) meeting. If practical, enforceable agreements can be worked out between nations, everyone will benefit.

3. Arthur Larson, an official in the Eisenhower administration, has suggested creation of a cabinet-level department of peace. This could be a superficial nothingness or something substantial, depending on the emphasis an administration gives it, and upon the traditions the department would develop. But a cabinet-level office which would look at the arms race, at trade regulations, at foreign aid, and at other concerns which are the direct responsibility of another department might be a healthy thing.

4. We must create an atmosphere in which political leaders can reduce arms production. McGeorge Bundy, the former presidential adviser, said in an article: "I know of no escape from the conclusion that both in his sensible abhorrence of nuclear conflict and his persistent attachment to still more weapons systems the political leader is reflecting his constituency. The fault lies less in our leaders than in ourselves." *

Possibilities for action:

1. Write to the United States State Department for the latest information on progress, if any, on disarmament.

2. Write to your congressman and senator and tell him

* "To Cap the Volcano." *Foreign Affairs*, October, 1969.

you favor strengthening the United Nations and that you favor responsible moves which can be made toward disarmament.

3. Get together six of your friends who may share these concerns. Then write to your congressman or senator and tell him that the next time he is in your area you would like 15 minutes of his time to discuss the disarmament problem. When you meet with him, be sure to listen as well as talk. (If he won't meet with you, you will have learned something about your congressman.)

TRADE

Your grandfather or great-grandfather perhaps sat around a pot-bellied stove in a small general store and argued about tariffs. At one time it was the dominant issue on the national political scene. Today it has become so complicated that few understand it, but it is not less important.

The tendency to protectionism—to keep foreign products from coming into the United States—is understandable. But caution must be exercised in any restraints on free trade, for restraints more likely will hurt the United States' economy rather than help it. Nations whose products cannot be sold in our country because of tariff regulations or import quotas may not allow United States' products to be sold to their people. We are hurt because we cannot sell, and because our own products may cost more than those from abroad.

Much more important, the pressure for higher tariffs and greater restrictions plays havoc with the economies of the smaller, developing nations of the world. A business which has been developed within one of these smaller countries can be eliminated almost overnight by the capricious action of the United States government.

For example, a few years ago the United States suddenly increased the tariff on clothespins. Apparently importing of clothespins from Denmark was hurting the domestic clothespin market. But when the United States did that, it not only hurt that particular business in Denmark, it also, in effect, told investors in Costa Rica and Kenya and Surinam: "You better think twice about investing your money in building up your country. The United States may suddenly put you out of business." Too much of the limited wealth in these developing countries goes to banks in the United States, Switzerland and Canada, rather than into the country which so desperately needs it.

Unfortunately the field of foreign trade is so complicated that fewer and fewer people pay much attention to it. Its importance far outweighs the attention it receives.

Possibilities for action:

1. Find out what the three largest industries are in your state and how international trade affects them. (Don't forget to include agriculture as an industry.)

2. Find out what legislation is before congress in these fields and how your congressman voted on international trade measures.

FOREIGN AID

If the problem with trade is that it is not understood, the problem with foreign aid is that it is understood incorrectly. The public image of foreign aid is of money being poured down the drain, money from the United States which helps only those already rich and powerful, and does little for the average citizen in the recipient country.

While the handling of foreign aid has not been perfect,

it has been a program United States citizens should view with pride, for it has helped many millions who were in desperate need of help, and it has been a major factor in developing our own economy.

After World War II, under the Marshall Plan the United States spent approximately 2½ per cent of our total national income on foreign aid. Today the most generous estimate is that we spend less than one-third of 1 per cent.

Why? Has poverty diminished around the world? Obviously not. Has the income of United States citizens diminished? No. Then why have we so drastically reduced this expenditure?

After World War II, your congressman could go back to his district and tell the Schmidts, "I'm helping your relatives in Germany." He could tell the Hansens, "I'm helping your relatives in Denmark." He could tell the Zaganellis, "I'm helping your relatives in Italy." And on and on. In other words, more than two decades ago, a congressman made votes back home by favoring foreign aid.

Now he would lose votes because the people who need help today live in India and Guatemala and Pakistan—and they don't have many relatives in his district.

The distinguished British economist, Barbara Ward Jackson, has suggested that all of the relatively wealthy nations of the world should devote 1 per cent of their income to helping the developing nations. This makes economic sense; as nations develop, their governments and their people can purchase our products.

It also makes sense in terms of simple humanity. Men cannot live on $60 a year (and many must live on much less than that) with any sense of pride, dignity, and hope.

It also makes sense in terms of survival, for the people of the United States cannot survive in a world in which the rich are getting richer and the poor are getting poorer.

Possibilities for action:

1. Write your congressman. Tell him you favor more economic assistance—not military assistance—to the poorer nations of the world. Get five of your friends to write, also.

2. Plan now to take a trip to an out-of-the-way corner of the world within five years, using either personal savings or by joining the Peace Corps or a similar group. When you travel, keep your eyes and heart open. Don't be a typical tourist.

3. Start now to read about just one country among the developing nations. Learn its economic problems. Write to that country's ambassador in Washington and ask for information. Perhaps he would visit your community and speak to a group there.

4. Take advantage of the opportunity to visit with foreign students in the United States—but remember that a student from another country does not necessarily reflect public opinion in his country any more than a student in our country does. In addition, remember that some foreign students come from upper income homes and may not understand the problems of others in their nation who face great obstacles.

Agriculture

The problem of agriculture is placed with subjects of international concern because long-range solutions to our own agricultural problems cannot be separated from the international scene.

These are the three fundamental realities:

1. Somewhere between 10,000 and 15,000 people on the face of the earth die each day from malnutrition.

2. The United States farmer has become so efficient that we now have what many people call "excess production," and so we are paying for the non-production of about one out of every six acres of productive farm land in the United States.

3. The farmer has not shared fully in the general prosperity of the nation.

We have tried to solve the last two problems without recognizing their relationship to the first. This must change, for there really is no excess food production in the world today—only a miserable system of distribution. We must unclog the avenues of distribution as best we can—and develop a domestic farm program that does not keep food from people who need it.

We cannot simply produce all that we can and then dump it on the foreign market, nor can we simply tell the American farmer he is to have no help or protection from government.

The answer must lie in devising policies which encourage production, which stimulate the channels of distribution, and which help the efficient family farmer. The billions now spent on farm programs do none of these things well —and that has been true of farm programs of both political parties in recent years.

The theory behind the non-production program is that it saves the soil. The fact is that today we have enough technical competence to produce year after year on the same land without impairing the soil, and with fertilizers which will not add to our environmental problems.

I believe that a sensible program can be worked out at considerably less cost than the present program. Finding an answer is imperative, both for the sake of the people who need food and for the sake of the farmer caught in the economic squeeze.

Because of the population growth we can anticipate in the immediate future, finding an answer cannot wait indefinitely. Agricultural economists with a sense of the world picture can contribute much. But so must farmers—old and young—and all of us who want to live in a stable world.

Agricultural policy today is much too important to be the concern of only one segment of our economy.

Possibilities for action:

1. Talk to some farmers so that you will understand their problems.

2. If possible, spend a few weeks of your summer vacation working on a farm. You will learn to appreciate more fully what a farmer has to do.

3. Study United States agricultural policies in light of the total world food situation. If you believe the present policies need to be changed, let your congressman know—and let others know also.

The United Nations

This relatively young international agency has many weaknesses and defects. So did the United States when it was 25 years old. But the alternative to international cooperation is international chaos.

The distinguished anthropologist, Margaret Mead, believes that part of the turmoil among young people today is caused by the fact that for perhaps the first time in history, there is a greater sense of belonging to the entire world community, rather than to just one nation.

Hopefully the time will come when the United Nations' ability to deal with a military situation can be strengthened. This would make it possible for all nations to devote more of their energies to non-armament production, to creating things which will help man and not harm him.

From time-to-time the United Nations does things with which we do not agree, but that is also true of our own government. We do not tear down our own government because we differ on something—nor should we do so with international government.

The strengthening process will be slow, and it will require the support of men of good will of every faith and nation. If anti-United Nations sentiment should dominate the world scene, I believe that a global war of unbelievable dimensions would be an almost certain result.

Your voice and mine should be one of support.

Possibilities for action:

1. Find out where the nearest chapter of the United Nations Association is and consider joining.

2. Write to U. N. headquarters, United Nations, New York, and ask for background information about the U. N.

3. Learn enough about the United Nations so that when someone says it is not effective or is just not working, you can point out the facts.

4. Let your congressman know that you favor strengthening the international policing arm of the United Nations.

5.

Domestic
Issues

The relationship of the United States with other nations and the special problems of our nuclear age are of tremendous importance, of course. But the problems we are facing within our own country are vital, too. Among the following issues are some that are of major concern to young people. They also are areas in which you might work most effectively for change.

The Draft

A substantial number of political and governmental leaders believe that the draft can be eliminated and that it is desirable to do so. All admit that this would be costly, but it could be done and it would unquestionably reduce some of the bitter divisions which plague the nation today.

But there are more serious problems than expense to be considered. There are many—I include myself among them —who feel that an all-volunteer military could represent a long-range threat to the nation, because history has shown us that most countries have not lost their freedom to an outside invader, but to an army takeover within. I vividly recall a 1967 visit with one of the Greek generals who engineered the overthrow of constitutional government there. He readily admitted knowing nothing about politics, although he was a high-ranking government official when he told me that. Greece had been having domestic problems which concerned all her citizens. A handful of military leaders were persuaded that there was only "one way to save the country," and that was for them to take over. I have no reason to doubt their sincerity. When a tense situation develops in most nations, it is always easy to persuade a few military leaders that they "have to save the country." Fortunately this has not been part of the United States' military tradition, but that could change.

The draft has major defects and those who "know the angles" generally can avoid it today. This is particularly true if you can make it into college.

One change would be to make the draft virtually universal for the male population at the age of 19, exempting only those with serious mental or physical handicaps. All who are drafted would have a choice of perhaps 10 areas of service to their country, and one of these areas would be the armed forces. Those who cannot read and write would no longer be exempt but would spend a portion of their service time learning these skills. Those who come into service without a marketable skill might also learn that. Among the choices would be the Peace Corps and Vista, for those who qualify; it might include working two years in a mental hospital.

This approach would keep the military from being all-volunteer. It would make the draft fairer, and it would help the colleges by removing those students who are there only to avoid the draft. In many cases, it also would bring to the campuses students with more maturity.

Possibilities for action:

1. Find out who is on your local draft board and how the board actually works. How were the members selected, and how often do they meet?

2. Go to the library and trace back for one year how many governments have been overthrown throughout the world. The international sections in such magazines as *Time* or *Newsweek* will give you this information. Then ask yourself these questions: Does the information you have gathered have any significance for our nation? Why was the military so often involved?

3. Determine in your own mind what our national policy should be on selective service. Get a few others who agree with you and then communicate your views to key people in Washington, including your congressman and senators.

4. Send a "Letter to the Editor" to the local newspaper, outlining your views, briefly and to the point.

Race

So much has been written in this area that these remarks will be brief. Those who like the status quo point to all that has been accomplished in the last two decades—and much has been done. Those who want change quickly point to all that needs to be done—and much needs to be done. Both are correct, in pointing to progress and pointing to need.

So long as there is need, so long as there is unfairness, so long as there is a deep-seated feeling on the part of one-ninth of the nation that they are not fully a part of the nation, action must be taken. But those of us who seek more action must put it into perspective. We must point to what has happened, as well as to what must take place, so that bitterness does not deepen.

The morning newspaper has an ad: "New two-bedroom homes for sale, $200 down, $95 a month for 30 years." (The last words—*for 30 years*—were in small print.) Everyone knows that the area advertised is for whites only. It would be illegal to put that in an ad, but it's not necessary; we all know. Yet some of the greatest housing needs in our country are for our black citizens.

When the news media note a rise in unemployment to 5.1 per cent, that means as much as 20 per cent in some black areas, sometimes because of "last hired, first fired" traditions, but also because of inadequate educational opportunities, lack of transportation to job markets, migration from rural areas to the cities, and other factors.

Whatever the domestic problem—medical services, unemployment, education, housing, environment—it afflicts the American of African heritage more than it does the American of European heritage. The answer lies in solving the problems so that all of us can move ahead.

Unfortunately—as the Kerner Commission report points out in detail—divisions within the country at times appear to be widening, rather than closing. One of the reasons for the sometimes deepening divisions is the tendency of all people—black and white—to read a statement by an extremist of one side or another and to believe that what he says represents the opinion of his racial group about another. Disraeli, the great nineteenth century British statesman, described the industrially developing England as "two nations between whom there is no intercourse and no sympathy; who are as ignorant of each other's habits, thoughts and feelings, as if they were dwellers in different zones or inhabitants of different planets." His description of the division between economic classes in England sounds too accurate for comfort in our black-white situation. Hopefully, we will have the good sense to improve the situation.

It should be added that a sizable and rapidly growing ethnic group which sometimes faces even more difficulties is the Spanish-speaking group, chiefly the Mexicans, Puerto Ricans, and, in some areas, Cubans. They face many of the same problems Afro-Americans face and, in addition, there is the barrier of language. In Illinois the highest school drop-out rate exists not among the blacks, but among the Spanish-speaking groups. The smallest percentage (relative to the population) of students in our colleges and universities comes from the Spanish-speaking community. Their problem is aggravated by the fact that in Illinois there is no one of Mexican or Puerto Rican background on the Chicago city council or in the state legislature. Their spokesmen have to be those of us who have never shared most of the difficulties they have experienced.

Gregory Miranda, one of the Puerto Rican leaders, has expressed the feelings of many: "If we would riot, people would pay attention to us. How bad do our problems have to get before people pay attention to them?"

But the dominant racial problem still is that facing the nation's black citizens. A group called the Black Christian Students of Chicago, at 720 North Rush Street, publishes a mimeographed monthly magazine called *Soul Power*. In the July, 1970, edition is a poem by Lelia Carter which summarizes the feeling of many:

Why Bother?
I am tired of waiting for tomorrow to come,
Knowing it will not be the same or better than today.

It seems ridiculous to wait so long,
Since there'll be no difference anyway.
I really have no reason to smile
   and I'm too darned tired to cry—
I'm sick of being tired.
Disgusted of asking why.
The dawn of the future doesn't look any brighter.
The shadows of the past draw tighter and tighter.
I cannot fight the dark to find the light.
I greet the new day wishing
   last night had been my Last Night.

Perhaps Harry Mark Petrakis has told the tragic truth about all of us in his recently published book, *Stelmark*: "In the midst of multitudes we exist like barricaded islands, fearful or unwilling to reveal ourselves or to discover the meaning of others." *

Possibilities for action:

1. Find out what minority group in your community faces the most difficult problems. Ask yourself how many friends you have among them, and why don't you have more. Help to create a situation where you and perhaps some others can have a good, frank exchange of views with a number of young people within that minority group.

2. If you have no easily definable minority groups in your community, find the reason. Explore the special problems or attitudes within your community and see what can you do to improve them.

3. Discuss with some of the clergy of your community

* *Stelmark* by Harry Mark Petrakis, David McKay, New York, 1970.

the problems of race as they exist, and determine with them what can be done to improve the situation.

4. Study employment patterns in your community and in your county, both by government and by private industry. Do job opportunities exist equally for black and white? Are promotions given to minority group members?

Poverty

George Romney, secretary of housing and urban development, points out that at the end of the nineteenth century, 90 per cent of the nation lived below the poverty level; today it is only 15 per cent. He also states that ours is the first nation in history with the majority of its population "reasonably well off." (The accuracy of the latter depends on what you consider "reasonably well off.")

In any event, almost one out of eight citizens lives at an undesirably low economic level, according to 1970 figures from the federal office of economic opportunity. In the wealthiest nation on earth, that is neither desirable nor necessary. But the figures are cold and impersonal. They do not convey the bitterness of a mother who knows her children are sick because she cannot feed them adequately. They do not express the terror of wondering whether you can feed your children because you had to buy expensive medicine for one of them who became desperately ill. A recent book on poverty, *Living Poor* by Moritz Thomsen, published by the University of Washington Press, says the condition of poverty "is like being sentenced to exist in a stormy sea in a battered canoe, requiring all your strength simply to keep afloat; there is never any question of reaching a destination."

The most dramatic illustrations of poverty are in our cities, but poverty does not exist only in the cities. In wealthy states such as Pennsylvania and Illinois, there are all-white rural areas where unemployment is high and where even those who are employed live at a marginal level.

In Pope County, Illinois, with a virtually all-white population, the economy has deteriorated to the point where fewer than 4,000 people still live there, and 14 per cent of them are on public aid. In nearby Pulaski County, 26 per cent of the population is on public aid. At the tip of southern Illinois lies the city of Cairo, generally neglected by the state through the years. Its great potential for industrial development has not been tapped. The biggest industry in the city starts employees at $1.60 an hour and more than 10 per cent of the employable population is out of work. The city is poor, and 20 per cent of the county is on public aid. One drive through the city tells you that. Because there are not enough dollars to go around, citizens have to struggle with one another for the dollars. Or they leave town, and too much of the community's potential leadership has done that. Cairo is 60 per cent white, 40 per cent black; racial incidents occur at least once a week. *If* the economic level of the community could be improved, many of the other problems would solve themselves—not overnight, but at least the direction of the community would be forward and not backward.

What can be done to reduce poverty within the United States?

1. As this is being written, President Nixon's proposal for a federal guarantee of income for families of four or more is tied up in committee in congress by an overwhelming negative vote. While the plan has some questionable points, it is a step forward, most experts believe, and an experiment at least worth trying.

2. We must recognize that the present public aid programs have, in large measure, been a failure, both to the taxpayer and to the recipients. People have been forced to eke out an existence without having their basic problems solved.

3. Federal standards for public aid would discourage the excessive moving about of families and lift the standard of assistance in areas where it is far below the level of livability. Under the present setup, a family from Arkansas can move to Illinois and overnight become eligible for more than twice as much public aid. The result is that people are moving to improve their economic circumstances, but this usually is not healthy for the nation or for the people. When a family arrives in Illinois or California or New York or Michigan—or you name the state—it is hard to find work and a place to live. Most of these families therefore move many times, creating educational problems for their children and long-range problems for society.

4. Approximately 34 per cent of those who fall below the poverty line are over 65, or are blind, or permanently and totally handicapped. Some type of guaranteed income for these people who in most instances cannot be expected to be substantial income producers would overnight eliminate one-third of the nation's poverty.

5. Some type of joint government-private enterprise guaranteed employment program should be set up, at least on an experimental basis. If Tom Smith has been unemployed for six months, perhaps government should say to a near-by steel company, "You put Tom Smith to work in your plant, and the first three months he works the government will pay one-half of his salary. For the next three months he works, we will pay one-fourth of his salary. By

that time you will have a trained employee and the responsibility for paying him will be entirely yours." Ultimately such a program would mean a saving both to the company and the taxpayer, and Tom Smith would be able to live with more pride.

6. Many of those who would benefit by jobs are not Tom Smiths, but Mrs. Tom Smiths. Day care centers to free them for employment must be expanded.

7. We must recognize that many who are unemployed either do not have good work habits or are people whose ability to hold a job is marginal at best. More one-day-at-a-time work opportunities must be created for them, as has been done to some extent in agricultural areas.

8. The areas with a high concentration of the poor unfortunately are generally the same localities with a high concentration of poor schools. The quality of the schools must be improved and adult education programs must be inaugurated and promoted.

9. Government and civic groups must cooperate more in locating industry in areas of high unemployment, particularly the rural areas where there is unemployment. For the cities, a more sensible program probably would be to improve transportation and housing opportunities in suburban areas where jobs are available.

The great challenge of poverty is not resources, but will.

Possibilities for action:

1. Find out what housing opportunities exist for families in your community who have limited incomes. Is inexpensive housing for the elderly available? If you are not satisfied with the answers you receive, write to your state's housing authority, tell them of your concern and ask what you can do about it.

2. Visit three families on public aid in your area. Why are they on public aid? What can be done to help them help themselves? Do they have any hope for the future? If not, why not?

3. Persuade your family to live for one week on the food allowance the same size family on public aid would receive. It will be quite an experience for your family.

4. Visit a poverty area in another county that differs from the poverty area you know.

5. Find out what legislation is pending in congress and in your state legislature which would affect the poor. Study it, then let your representatives know your views. If you feel strongly on a matter, get others to communicate with them, also.

POPULATION

As of 1970 the earth's population was approximately 3.5 billion people. By the year 2000 that figure is expected to rise to approximately 7 billion. Here is another way of putting it: From the beginning of time to the year 1970, 3.5 billion people have lived on this earth; in another 30 years, that figure will double. When you project beyond the year 2000—even by just one century—the population figures lead to conclusions which are too explosive to even think about.

If civilization as we know it is to be maintained, some means of stopping this alarming birth rate must be found. Within the United States, the birth rate has been reduced appreciably because of the existence of "'the pill," although it would be wrong to assume we have solved all of our population problems.

The great problem, however, lies beyond our borders and there solutions are both difficult and complicated. In India today, for example, a man is given a transistor radio if he agrees to voluntary sterilization. In India, where the average annual income is approximately $70, a transistor radio is a big thing. Despite this program and many others, the population keeps climbing dramatically, in large part because of economic reasons. The sons of a family are frequently that family's sole form of social security. If there are four sons, two may live to manhood, and then can help support their parents in their declining years.

While there are exceptions, generally the two most effective means of controlling population are a relatively high standard of living and a reasonably high level of education. In India, where approximately 75 per cent of the population is illiterate, conveying information about a good birth control program obviously is difficult.

With declining expenditures in foreign aid already plaguing government, the United States is reluctant to push birth control programs in other countries. Some nations resent it, just as do some people within the United States.

The environmental problem is directly related to the population problem. As we have more and more people, and as their income level gradually rises, we produce more and more for them to consume, and that means more air pollution, more water pollution, and more environmental problems.

Exactly how the United States and other nations will control population is not clear, but it is abundantly clear that action is needed quickly.

Possibilities for action:

1. You must think through a very personal question: the population crisis perhaps should have a bearing on how many children you will have.

2. Check into whether or not your state provides help for those who wish to limit their families.

MEDICAL SERVICE

Pembroke township in Illinois has 12,000 citizens and does not have a full-time physician. If you drive along Highway 66 (Interstate 55)—the main road from Chicago to St. Louis—you will see such signs as "Odell Needs a Doctor," "Divernon Needs a Doctor." Illinois schools graduated more physicians in 1934 than they did in 1970. When you consider our growing population, the number of physicians who go into research, and the number who go on to specialize, the net effect is substantially less service per capita than the state had in 1934. In 1930 the United States had one physician for 1,139 people; 40 years later we have one for 1,750.

The United States is first among nations in medical research; it is 18th among nations in life expectancy for a male; girls do a little better. The United States ranks 14th among nations in infant mortality rate at birth.

Not only is there a shortage of physicians, but their placement presents special problems. In the major cities, the areas with the highest incidence of disease, injury and crime-related accidents—the ghetto areas—are also the areas with the smallest number of physicians per person.

A similar problem faces us with dentists, both as to numbers and location. In East St. Louis, Illinois—about 70 per cent black—10 per cent of the dentists serve 70 per cent of the people; 90 per cent of the dentists serve 30 per cent of the people.

While figures for the entire nation are not comforting, the statistics of survival in the inner city are alarming. In slum areas there is "three times as much heart disease, five times as much mental disease, four times as much high blood pressure, and four times as many deaths before age thirty-five than there is nation-wide." *

Not long ago the American Medical Association fought attempts to deal with the shortage of physicians. Happily that picture has now changed and the American Medical Association is showing some leadership to help solve the problem. An article by their president, published in the *Reader's Digest* in 1970, dramatically pointed out the need.

It is not only a problem of having enough physicians, it is also a question of how we can guarantee to everyone the opportunity for good medical service within the ability to pay.

To have the finest research available, but not be able to use it because of inadequate manpower or the inability of some citizens to pay for it, means hope for some and hopelessness for others.

Possibilities for action:

1. Find out if there are areas in your county without adequate medical services. If so, what is your state doing to help in this situation?

2. Talk to someone you know who has had major medical problems within the last year. Find out how those costs were financed. Talk to a physician; ask his opinion on what can and should be done to meet the heavy medical expenses some people face.

3. Find out what bills are pending in congress as you read this. You can get this by writing to your congressman, House Office Building, Washington, D. C. After you know

* "Paying More, Getting Less," by Fred Anderson. *The New Republic*, January 17, 1970.

the general provisions of these bills, if one seems to make sense to you, start a letter-writing campaign in its behalf.

Air Pollution

Every five years between 1950 and 1970, the deaths caused by bronchitis and emphysema have doubled in the United States. A friend of mine had chest pains regularly and thought he had heart trouble, but tests were negative. His physician suggested that the one-hour drive to work every day and the one-hour drive home might have something to do with it because of the fumes he breathed. Two years ago he moved from the city to a smaller community and his chest pains disappeared.

Not too many years ago, even the term "air pollution" was not known in legal circles. We talked some about smoke abatement, but suddenly we have become more aware of the problems of such cities as London and Los Angeles, as well as smaller cities and communities. Fifteen years ago I would drive through Wood River, Illinois, with its oil refineries and strong odors, and believe that what I smelled was an essential part of a refinery. Now we know differently. Fifteen years ago I received complaints from residents near the steel mills and when I visited these people, I saw that air pollution from the refinery had peeled much of the paint from their homes. Yet, I did not fully realize what those same fumes could do to the lungs of human beings.

The greatest cause of damage from air pollution is voluntary: the cigarette you may smoke. Government cannot do much more to discourage you—although subsidizing tobacco growers and paying for films promoting tobacco, while at the same time warning people that it causes death, seem grossly inconsistent.

The next greatest cause of air pollution is the automobile. In most large cities, cars cause between 47 and 90 per cent of the air pollution. Research on different types of engines is going on behind the scenes, and starting with many of the 1972 cars, the combustion engine should produce appreciably less pollution. Manufacturers and processors of gasoline have made some progress in producing lead-free gasoline, and more progress in reducing pollutants is expected. Ironically, right now in Illinois automobile plants are producing two types of cars—one for shipment to California, and the other for sale in Illinois and other states. The California model is more pollution-free than the car for Illinois and other states. I am happy for California, but regret that our state, where many of these cars are produced, is not protecting its citizens as well as California. Government generally has done less than industry. I have seen black smoke belching from the Troy Grade School, one block from my home; I have seen it coming from the Von Steuben High School in Chicago, and from Springfield's municipal power plant.

Because pollution remains a part of the earth's atmosphere, efforts for clean air must be pursued vigorously, both by the United States and other nations.

A group of grade school students sent me a petition in behalf of clean air. The petition was headed: "Give Us This Day Our Daily Breath."

That's not asking too much.

Possibilities for action:

1. If you see thick, black smoke coming from the smokestack of a factory or government building in your area, write to your state's air pollution control agency and report it. Find out what is being done.

2. Find out if your state's regulations on automobiles and airplanes are as strict as those in other states. If they are not, perhaps you should initiate some letters to the governor and legislators, and to your local newspaper about the situation.

3. Write to a leading medical school in your state and ask someone who is an expert in respiratory diseases how he evaluates your state's efforts in combating air pollution.

WATER POLLUTION

Most traditional forms of animal life no longer live in Lake Erie or in many smaller lakes throughout the nation. Many of the traditionally beautiful rivers and streams now are so polluted that visitors wonder what could possibly have inspired the writers who serenaded them.

For the second summer in a row, many communities along Lake Michigan have posted notices that it is not safe to use the lake along their beaches. After his recent crossing of the Atlantic in a replica of an ancient Egyptian boat, Thor Heyerdahl said that the crew did not see man often, but they saw his garbage all the time. Some coastal communities have learned dramatically that water and oil do not mix, for oil spills have ruined beaches and killed many birds and fish.

As the demand for water grows, and our need for disposal of sewage and trash also increases, the need to take extreme care in preserving the available water supplies and keeping them clean multiplies.

Not only municipal and industrial plants must be carefully policed, but care also must be taken as to what sprays are used to control insects, because these insecticides eventually are washed out of plants and soil into our rivers and oceans.

In addition, all of us must use more self-restraint as to what is thrown into a river or lake or ocean. To see ships and small boats use the water as a huge garbage can is to see mankind acting with sickening lack of vision. To see a city use the ocean as a garbage dump, as I did recently, is to wonder if man's thinking process functions at all. Citizens who camp or walk over a bridge and toss cigarette wrappers or milk cartons into streams share in the guilt of mauling our environment.

Self-restraint is essential for self-preservation.

Possibilities for action:

1. Get a friend or two to join you on a canoe or small boat trip down the nearest river or stream where it would be safe for you to travel. As you move down the river, note what waste disposal you see. If there are people, companies or municipalities polluting the water, note the exact time and place and report it to officials. After you have made your trip down the river, carefully observing what is happening, write a story for your local newspaper. If you can take pictures along the way, this would be helpful, both for the story and to secure legal action to stop the pollution.

2. Following essentially the plan indicated above, do the same thing, only make it a walking tour.

3. Write to your state water control agency and ask those in charge whether your local community's water, sewer and sewage treatment programs meet acceptable standards. If the answer is "No," discuss it with local officials and civic leaders, and decide on a plan to improve standards.

NOISE POLLUTION

Less talked about than air and water pollution is noise pollution, but you will be reading much more about it.

At least one million workers in the United States have suffered some serious loss of hearing because of excessive noise where they work. Estimates are that between seven and 17 million of our people work under conditions that contribute to a loss of hearing. Teenagers who work in rock bands frequently have the hearing of a person of 65.

But it is not only hearing that is impaired.

Studies in this country show that an animal's life span is shortened when the noise level regularly goes above certain levels. A study made in Germany shows that the noise of boiler factories, railroad stations, and airports may stunt growth and weaken the hearts of children who live in the area. Canadian experiments demonstrate that loud sounds have given rats ulcers and sometimes have driven them crazy—literally.

What happens when you hear a loud noise? Your system automatically protects itself by sending blood rushing to your head. Your blood pressure is increased, as is the heart rate, and the blood sugar level rises. When these changes take place too often—as they may for people working in a steel mill or living next to a subway—abnormal brain patterns and other neural disturbances can develop, as well as heart trouble.

Not only medical experts are concerned about the problem. The National Geographic Society is taking a serious interest in what it calls "sonic sickness." A recent press release from the Society notes:

"Experts warn that the world is getting twice as noisy every ten years. Many European nations are far ahead in muffling noise pollution. . . . Progressive industries and unions are cooperating to protect factory workers' ears and shorten the time they must spend with loud machinery.

Business leaders now see coffee breaks as needed escapes from the clattering typing pool where fatigue may cause half of all typing errors. Sound-soaking drapes, ceilings, partitions, and carpets are standard in most offices. . . . Steelworkers have turned up with 'hopscotch' heartbeats, mill hands have developed abnormal brainwaves, men in boiler factories have complained about bad circulation. Unmuffled tractors harvest the hearing of many farmers. . . . The problem, say doctors, is too much noise hitting the ear too long, affecting nerves and blood vessels. People have just become too used to noise, laments one physician. 'It might be a good thing if noise made people's ears bleed,' he said. 'Then they'd get more interested in quiet.' "

Many municipalities have banned the use of the automobile horn, but much more needs to be done to reduce noise. The problem is more pressing in congested areas. There even are some who believe that there is a relationship between the crime rate and the noise level in urban areas. In any event, the noise level must be reduced, not for the sake of comfort, but for the sake of health.

Possibilities for action:

1. Since this is a relatively new field, literature and programs are just beginning to appear. You can read about the research, and then follow up on what should be done in your community.

2. Take a look at your own home, and at your car. Are there places where you can reduce noise? When you play a record, or have the radio or TV on, can you turn down the volume? Does your car have a noisy muffler?

3. What are the major sources of noise in your community? What can be done to reduce the noise level?

Narcotics and Marijuana

Almost everyone—including those addicted—agrees that hard narcotics do great damage to the human mind and body. The death rate, for example, of those in their twenties who are users of hard narcotics is approximately the same as it is for men in their seventies. No one knows how many burglaries have been committed for narcotics, or how many girls have become prostitutes to support their addiction. The chamber of horrors goes on and on, and the increase in the use of hard drugs is dramatic, if the statistics can be believed, though in some communities there appears to be reduced use.

Marijuana seems to be less harmful, immediately, to the body than the hard narcotics, though knowledge here is limited. Most who have been involved in the limited research on marijuana agree however that it *does* harm the body and perhaps the mind, but the extent of the damage is less clearly established. Because it is the "in" thing to do at some parties and in some areas, the number of people using marijuana is rising even more dramatically than the numbers of those using hard drugs. One does not automatically lead to the other, though most of those on hard drugs began by using marijuana. Smoking marijuana also can become habit-forming, though the habit is more easily broken than it is with the hard narcotics. Marijuana may not be physically addictive, but it can be psychologically addictive.

One of the difficulties with marijuana is that there are many varieties. A mild variety may do a person little damage, but the next time he may smoke a different variety and find himself "stoned" after the first drag.

Another difficulty is that, in their zeal to warn against marijuana, some adults have exaggerated the effects with the result that young people just do not believe that there is any danger.

Because marijuana is illegal, research has been difficult, though that is hardly a good argument for legalization. The effects of marijuana on the lungs, for example, is being tested as this is being written. It may adversely affect hearing and the central nervous system. *Newsweek* for September 7, 1970, summed up the situation: "Most medical authorities go along with the American Medical Association which brands marijuana 'a dangerous drug and as such a public-health concern.' " The National Institute of Mental Health which has done some of the research in this field has stated that, pending further study, marijuana "must be considered a risk to the mental and physical health of users."

Should it be legalized?

There are many young people who feel that it should be, though most of the experts who have studied the problem tend to oppose legalization. If the use of tobacco were just starting today, and we knew the full extent of the damage cigarettes do, would I vote to legalize the sale of cigarettes? I don't know; I doubt it. Obviously, we are long past consideration of the question of tobacco, but we are not past it on marijuana.

The use of marijuana must be limited as much as possible until more extensive research can be done, but early indications are that research will find that marijuana does do substantial harm.

What can be done in the meantime?

1. Educational programs about the well-established harmful effects of hard narcotics and the probable harmful effects of marijuana must be stepped up. The experience in

New York City, which has the best educational program, has been that former addicts who are still young can reach a high school or college audience much more effectively than anyone else.

2. Greater appropriations are needed for research on hard narcotics and on marijuana. We pay dearly for our failure to move ahead rapidly on research.

3. Penalties for the possession or use of marijuana must not be as harsh as those for hard drugs. When the law demands penalties which are too heavy, judges simply find defendants not guilty. Also, young people who have tried "pot" with no immediate, apparent harm, sometimes are led to believe that hard drugs are not dangerous, either, since the law equates marijuana with hard drugs.

4. Generally, those who use either hard narcotics or who use marijuana regularly do so as an emotional crutch. We must not only stop their use, but identify the emotional problems and deal with them.

Possibilities for action:

1. Have the courage to say "No" to anyone who wants to get you involved with drugs.

2. Check to see what your state offers in the way of a drug educational program. Does it seem adequate?

3. Write to your state's department of health and find out what type of program they have for those already addicted to drugs. Does the head of the department think it is a good program and adequately financed?

CONSERVATION

An excuse can always be found for destroying some wooded area. There is always a good reason for reducing the size of a forest preserve or a state park. Special interests can put forth many reasons why some of the nation's basic resources should be turned over to them for a small fee.

But with the population growing, the need for open space and wooded areas is growing also.

There must be many more small efforts to save a spot along a river or a lake, to preserve some sand dunes or to keep some rural wooded area relatively untouched. Most of these areas are prime targets for housing or industrial developments—and understandably there is real pressure for this sort of thing in a community. In most cases, however, open fields could be used just as easily for housing development as those areas which have greater conservation potential.

This is particularly important in metropolitan areas. During the next 50 years, the population of the Greater Chicago area, for example, will grow from approximately seven million to between 10 and 12 million. Unless there are people of vision in that area who will set land aside now, it soon will be too late and much too expensive to preserve the open spaces.

Another land grabber can be the highways. The engineers who design the highways also hold the hearings on whether or not their designs are good—and not surprisingly, their answer is almost always "Yes." Obviously, new highways do take more land, but sometimes improvement and upgrading of existing highways would consume less land and save a great deal of money. In New York State, a special commission reviews highway policies in order to fend off the unnecessary gobbling-up of land.

A regular program to preserve and expand your state's holdings of land to be used for conservation purposes is important.

Possibilities for action:

1. Visit your nearest state park. What is good about it? What are its greatest needs? How far do you have to go to get there?

2. Look at a map and mark an area 50 miles from where you live. Are there places within that 50-mile radius where a good state park could be developed, or at least a wooded area could be preserved?

3. Find out what type of park and recreational program your local community or county has. How does its program compare with other communities of similar size and population?

4. Write a letter to your legislators telling them you favor setting aside more land for conservation purposes.

5. Be willing to join local efforts to save natural, wooded areas.

CRIME

According to a Gallup Poll, 50 per cent of the nation's women and 19 per cent of the nation's men "would be afraid to walk alone at night" within a mile of where they live. More than all the statistics on murder, rape and burglary, this tells us that fear is a major force in the United States today.

In Rome, during all of 1968, there were a total of 14 murders. Chicago, a city of approximately the same size, has an average of almost 14 murders a week. Any other major American city could be cited along with Chicago. The answer is not simply more police. The Chicago police under Superintendent James Conlisk have superior leadership, but many foreign observers believe our nation already has too many police. Adding more police in various communities does not drop the crime rate dramatically. One reason is that we expect too much of our police. We expect them to do what we have failed to do in our homes, schools, churches and government, to solve basic difficulties confronting our society.

Concern with crime is universal; it concerns people in the ghetto who are most frequently the victims of it, and it concerns those in the suburbs who, though less frequently subjected to its terror, see evidence of it on television and read about it in the newspapers.

The answer to the problem of crime is not solved by candidates for public office trying to outdo each other in screaming "law and order." *Everyone is for law and order; the question is not who is for it, but how it can be achieved.*

When a community has problems, they are reflected in its crime statistics. A community with a high rate of unemployment almost inevitably will have a high rate of crime. So will a community where racial tensions are high. If schools are bad, there likely will be a higher rate of crime. If people are packed together in undesirable housing, there will be a high rate of crime. If a community does not have a good recreational program, it may have a higher rate of crime. The litany could continue. When a community has problems, the problems must be faced honestly; when you can reduce the size of the problem, you almost inevitably will be reducing the size of crime.

Possibilities for action:

1. When you witness a crime, report it. Be willing to testify in court about what you saw. If more people did these two things, the incidence of crime would be reduced.

2. Check to see what the police in your area are being paid. If their pay is not adequate, you should support a

higher pay scale. Can the police retire at a reasonably early age? This is important, both to keep a force reasonably young and to help attract good men.

3. Find out about the prisons in your state. Prisons should be places of rehabilitation, not schools for crime. Unfortunately, most prisons in the United States are the latter. Approximately 95 cents out of every $1 spent in the prisons of the United States is for custodial services. Only five cents of each dollar is spent on rehabilitation. When someone is sent to prison, it should be with the reasonable hope that he will come out an improved citizen. That hope is not high in most areas of the United States today. A prisoner who goes into prison unable to read and write should come out with the ability to do so, if he is able to learn. If he does not have a marketable skill when he goes in, he should have one when he comes out so that he has a reasonable hope of "going straight." Our prison system is improving, but it has a long way to go.

4. In some areas strenuous efforts must be made to speed up the judicial process. "Justice delayed is justice denied," and that is true for society as well as for the person facing court actions. When prosecutors and courts fail to move with reasonable speed, innocent people must go about with a cloud over them, and the guilty may commit more crimes while they await court action.

5. Be careful in electing officials. If you elect a dishonest sheriff, district (or state's) attorney, or mayor, you can expect the laws to be openly violated, and you will reap the harvest in the decades ahead. All the programs in the world aren't worth the paper they are written on if voters put the wrong type of public official into office.

6. When public officials or public agencies do a good job, or if a citizen does a good job, be willing to commend

him. Some years ago, a leading underworld figure in our area threatened the life of the manager of the area telephone system. The telephone manager was August "Bud" Roller, a man in his early thirties who had a large family. Most people would have conveniently "forgotten" what was said. "Bud" Roller—a somewhat shy, retiring gentleman—does not look like a hero, but he is. He went before a grand jury to help put a stop to this. I wonder how many people ever thanked him.

I have been impressed by the conduct of the Illinois State Highway Police. How often do they receive a letter commending them? I don't know, but I would guess not often. A word of encouragement to people who do a good job for you could mean a great deal to them.

7. It should be added that there are no easy, simple answers to reducing crime. It is going to be hard, slow work, and anyone who tells you differently either does not know the facts, or is deceiving you. But on a very personal level, you can make a beginning by seeking out someone in your community who appears to be headed for trouble and trying to be of help.

THE MENTALLY ILL AND THE MENTALLY RETARDED

It is an oversimplification, but one with considerable truth, that there are two gauges of good government: First, is it honest? Second, is it willing to help the helpless?

In perhaps no other area is there a clearer test of the second question than in how we care for the mentally ill and the mentally retarded.

Part of our problem is the public attitude, still much too prevalent, that there is a stigma attached to someone with a relative who is mentally ill or retarded. Perhaps the majority of those with close relatives in this situation still feel some degree of shame. There should be no more shame attached to having a brother who is mentally retarded than in having a brother with a broken leg; there should be no more shame in having a father who is mentally ill than in having a father who has cancer.

Because of the public attitude, relatives of the mentally ill and retarded do not respond in the same way as do the relatives of people with cancer. It is true that there are Mental Health Associations, but considering the number of mentally ill in our society, the membership of these associations is relatively small.

The result is that pressure for adequate programs for the mentally ill and the retarded is not always great, and states respond to these needs inconsistently, moving ahead when there is a sympathetic governor, but otherwise doing little.

In most states, programs for the mentally ill are not good, and those for the mentally retarded are worse. What happens when someone in your community has mental or emotional problems? Are facilities available to help him there? If he has to be hospitalized (and many should not be), what is the condition of your state's public hospitals, compared with the private hospitals?

Or take the case of Uncle Fred who lives in your home. He is your mother's uncle, and because other relatives are not able to care for him, he has been with you for two years. He has the usual ailments advancing years bring, and he is at times forgetful. One day he goes downtown to get some pipe tobacco and a few other small things and gets lost. He can't find his way home and does not remember the address. About 8 o'clock that evening, after frantic calls to the police, they bring him home. Your parents don't know what to do. No one is at home during most of the day, since both of your parents work and you and your sister are in school. He could be placed in a home for the aged, but that would mean a real financial struggle for your family. The least expensive answer for your family is to send him to a state institution for the mentally ill, and that's what your parents do.

Unfortunately, Uncle Fred does not belong there because he really is not mentally ill. For most mental hospitals in the nation, approximately 30 per cent of their patients are Uncle Freds, older citizens who simply suffer from some senility. It is tragic for these aged citizens, and it is even more damaging to the other patients who are genuinely mentally ill, but who are denied the help they should have because so much time is spent simply providing custodial care for the aged.

In most states, the majority of the mentally retarded who could be helped are not. When I was first elected to the Illinois legislature, only 19 per cent of the educable and trainable mentally retarded were being educated by our public schools. Now that figure is close to 100 per cent—though the quality of help is frequently far from what it should be. It is still true in most states that local school boards are assumed to be responsible for the "normal" students, while those who are retarded, or hard of hearing, or disturbed are not being helped. Obviously that should change—if only from a viewpoint of dollars and cents; if we fail to help these young people, they eventually will become wards of the state. All of us will be paying for their care, while instead they could be leading more productive and happy lives. Hopefully our motivation can be on a higher plane than the economic level, because these people need and deserve help.

For those who must be placed in state institutions, the facilities and quality of care often are disheartening. A visit to one of your state's institutions for the mentally retarded might be a real eye-opener for you.

Providing or failing to provide help for the mentally ill and the retarded should tell us something about ourselves and whether we are or are not a civilized people.

Possibilities for action:

1. Visit an institution for the mentally ill. Visit an institution for the retarded, contacting the superintendent in advance. Ask perhaps six of your friends to join you on your visits. When you are there talk to employees and patients and ask them what improvements are needed. After your visits, discuss among yourselves what should be done to improve the situation.

2. Visit a private institution for the mentally ill and for the mentally retarded. Is there a great difference between the private and public places and should there be that much difference? What can be done to improve the situation?

3. Join a Mental Health Association or an Association for the Retarded—or both—in your area.

Cultural Programs

If you look at the appropriations of state governments, you may think that our civilization ultimately will be judged by the ribbons of concrete with which we brutalize our landscape. If you look at the federal budget, it would appear that the most important thing we believe our government should do is build weapons of destruction.

Only a small fraction of a state or federal budget goes toward encouraging the arts. Yet a few centuries from now we may be remembered in great part for our cultural contributions.

In most countries of the world you can listen to the finest symphony orchestras for a few cents. I have had excellent seats in some of the great musical halls of the world for 30 cents in United States money. When you compare these prices with what is charged to attend a concert by an American symphony orchestra, you understand why only a small percentage of our population ever develops a real interest in good music. Orchestras in other countries are subsidized, while in the United States orchestras struggle— frequently unsuccessfully—to make ends meet on their own. Sometimes they stage contrived programs to raise money. In St. Louis, Missouri, a professional football game helps finance the St. Louis Symphony. A look at a budget of any governmental unit shows that we think a symphony orchestra is not important.

Many other forms of art could be mentioned.

When I served in the army I was stationed for 13 months in Coburg, Germany. Its population then was less than 40,000, but Coburg had a tax-supported professional opera company and orchestra. You could go to the opera house and for a small sum hear the great works of music performed at prices any resident of Coburg could afford.

I think that the finest museum in the world—for visual excitement—is not located in the United States, but in Mexico. It is the Museum of Anthropology. Mexico's encouragement of the arts is apparent to anyone who drives through the country, and occasionally is startled and pleased to see a statue or work of art erected by the government in the most unexpected places.

There are good museums in the United States, but they are struggling to stay alive. Recently, I toured the Field Museum of Chicago, one of the finest in the United States, with Leland Weber, its director. He pointed to exhibits that remained uncleaned because the museum could not afford to clean them. The state of Illinois gives the museum not one penny. Today the museum operates with fewer custodians than it had 10 years ago, though attendance has increased almost 40 per cent.

There are some good, small cultural programs at universities, colleges, high schools, and sometimes these are sponsored by governmental units. Springfield, Illinois, has an excellent municipal chorus whose expenses are covered by a small municipal tax. Many communities have municipal bands. Several states have arts councils, but their budgets reflect community indifference rather than concern.

The artist who is also a good promoter can survive in our society. The artist who is only a good artist faces real difficulties.

Possibilities for action:

1. Does your state have an arts council? What is its appropriation and how does it compare with the state's budget?

2. Are there practical ways to bring cultural programs—symphony concerts, for example—to areas of the state and to areas of the bigger cities that they do not now reach?

3. Visit a museum in your state. Ask the director what his budget is and what it was 10 years ago. Get his comments on the adequacy of the budget.

The Urban Problem

I have said that all of these problems are inter-related. Much of what we consider the urban problem has been referred to in the sections on crime, poverty, race, pollution and population.

However, cities have a special problem which is particularly difficult. There seems to be a deep-seated desire on the part of many—including those who live near an urban center—to avoid facing any realities about the city. In one of its recent editorial essays, *Time* magazine noted that the new isolationism in the United States is not so much a desire to withdraw from foreign countries, but to "withdraw from New York: Lindsayland and the other big U. S. cities are more alarming now than the jungles of Indochina or the wilds of Europe. The world overseas represents almost an escape from America."

When we massively stockpile people into depersonalized situations, we create problems, whether it is a big city or a big university. And when these problems of density and depersonalization are compounded by other problems, the results can be explosive.

Take housing as an example. Every major city in the United States has a serious housing problem. Not many years ago, we thought that if the people living in dilapidated slum residences could simply be transferred to large, well-constructed high-rise apartment buildings, conditions would be greatly improved. And so the tall buildings were built; they even resembled the tall luxury apartment buildings near Lake Michigan in Chicago, or Central Park in New York. Many believed that this new, low-income housing could almost create a new city.

But problems quickly developed. The tall luxury buildings are filled chiefly with the wealthy and near-wealthy who have few or no children living in them. The same type of housing for the poor is swarming with children, and as the father of two small children I know how noisy and energetic children can be. This type of housing was not designed for children.

Low-cost housing also has segregated residents, both racially and economically. Most public housing is either all black or all white, though there may be a token representation of another racial group. The economic segregation may be worse. People who don't know how to solve their problems are stockpiled with others who don't know how to solve problems. The leavening effect of having school-age children come into contact with others of different cultural backgrounds is greatly reduced where the poor are concentrated. The result of these housing patterns has been better physical surroundings for many families, but they have been crowded into housing complexes where they sometimes live in fear because of inadequate police protection. Educational opportunities for young people are limited. People with high unemployment rates must live where there is no employment. And the hopes for new housing have been dashed, leading to deep frustration and resentment.

An especially difficult problem is the border area which is changing from all white to all black. The racial pattern of most large United States cities looks like this:

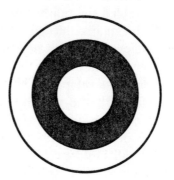

There is a high-rent area in the center of the city, near offices and the central business district, which is almost all white. Some of the more wealthy blacks live here, but not many. Then comes the big black belt, which in most cities is growing. That growth is limited by tradition—though no longer by law—to a ring around the white center. Small numbers of blacks, but no more than that, have been able to break into the nicer suburbs. The result is a white noose around the black belt of the central city. And in areas where that black central city has had to expand because of a growing population, there is serious friction—frequently aggravated by unscrupulous real estate dealers.

Recently a widow who lived in a small home in one of these changing neighborhoods was approached by a real estate salesman who painted a horrible picture of what was going to happen when blacks moved into the neighborhood. She became so frightened that she agreed to sell her home for $1,800, and he promptly sold it for more than 10 times that amount.

If integration remains a goal for our society—and I believe it is the only alternative to disintegration—then the white noose around the central city must be broken so that blacks who wish to live in more pleasant surroundings will have that opportunity.

This is but one example of a fact we have yet to face: The problem of the central city cannot be solved without the aid and cooperation of the suburban areas. Tragically, that cooperation is extremely limited. In part this arises from the fact that many who live in the suburbs moved there to get away from the city and they have an anti-city complex. They elect public officials who too often reflect the same bias. Those in the suburbs must realize that the survival of the city as a healthy entity is essential for the survival of the suburbs. More than three decades ago, George Bernard Shaw wrote:

"Such poverty as we have today in our great cities degrades the poor, and infects with its degradation the whole neighborhood in which they live. And whatever can degrade a neighborhood, can degrade a country and a continent and finally the whole civilized world, which is only a large neighborhood.

"Its bad effects cannot be escaped by the rich. When poverty produces outbreaks of virulent infectious disease, as it always does sooner or later, the rich catch the disease and see their children die of it. When it produces bad manners and bad language, the children of the rich pick them up, no matter how carefully they are secluded. The saying that we are members one of another is not a mere pious formula to be repeated in church without any meaning; it is a literal truth; for though the rich end of the town can avoid living with the poor, it cannot avoid dying with the poor.

"People will be able to keep themselves to themselves as much as they please when they have made an end of poverty; but until then they will not be able to shut out the sights and sounds and smells of poverty from their daily walks, not feel sure from day to day that its most violent and fatal evils will not reach them through their strongest police guards."

Possibilities for action:

1. If you do not live in a city, get a few friends to visit there with you. While you are there, see not only the traditional sights, but contact a church or social agency in advance of your visit and tell them you want to visit problem areas within the city so that you can better understand them.

2. Whether you live in a city or away from it, find out

what contact your area has with the problem areas of the city. What type of relationship should there be?

3. What are your state, your church, your school doing to help all citizens understand more clearly the problems of the city?

4. Bridges of understanding must be built between cities and suburban and rural areas. What can you do to help build such bridges?

5. Let your legislators know of your concern for the problems of the city.

EDUCATION

Books have been written and will be written on this subject, and it is presumptuous to try to add anything in a few paragraphs. But major goals in the field of education have yet to be fulfilled:

1. *We must have quality elementary and high school education for all young people in the nation.*

Most of our young people have this opportunity, but too many still are denied this right. Part of the reason is our excessive reliance on the real estate tax to raise revenue for educational purposes. The result is great inequities in the educational product. We no longer can tolerate inadequate education for anyone, for this aggravates all of our other social ills.

2. *Adult education programs must be improved, enlarged and made available in all communities.*

This is needed for the many who did not have a chance for a good education when they were younger; it also is needed for those who must develop new marketable skills, and it is important for the cultural enrichment of home and community. Adult education programs today have made only a beginning toward what they eventually must become.

3. *College programs should be as available to the poor as they are to the non-poor.*

While some young people undoubtedly are being pushed into college when they do not want to go or perhaps should not go, others still are not able to go to college because they do not have the money. A minimal program ought to call for greater assistance to banks to encourage low-interest loans to students. As of this writing, most banks are not making such loans. Pressure and help from government could change this quickly. We also should work out a form of direct subsidy—similar to the GI Bill for veterans— so that all students with ability will have the chance to go to college. It is an investment in our future.

4. *In urban areas, a means must be found to give people a greater voice in school affairs.*

Here we know more about what does not work than what does. What is clear is that urban education too often is not quality education and, perhaps related to that, people living near a school have little voice in what goes on in that school. Somehow making that school more responsive to the voice of the immediate community is necessary. How we can do this effectively and responsibly is not yet clear.

Possibilities for action:

1. Visit a teacher from a problem school and find out what he or she thinks must be done.

2. There are local educational organizations where you live. Find out who the officers are and ask for their organization's program for improving the schools in your state or community.

3. Find out how your community's adult educational

program compares with that of other communities. Remember that yours is not a good program if your community's program is weak and your neighboring community's program is weaker.

4. What is the major foreign-language group in your state or area? What help are they receiving from the schools?

INFLATION

This plagues all of us, but people with limited, fixed incomes suffer more than the rest of us. The cure includes a strong sense of direction by the federal government, including greater efforts to reduce interest rates and excessive expenditures.

State and local governments also bear a major share of the blame, for indebtedness by state and local governments is growing much more rapidly than indebtedness at the federal level. School districts generally have no choice but to create an indebtedness, and many local governments face the same dilemma.

States generally do have a choice, but they have avoided the simple but difficult method of financing their affairs on a pay-as-you-go basis. The result is not only inflationary, but it means that an increasingly high percentage of the tax dollar in state and local government goes for interest, rather than for goods and services. No one can argue seriously that this is healthy.

Diminishing the inflationary trend somewhat would be placing some sensible limitation on consumer credit. Credit cards should not be permitted to be mailed out unsolicited. More realistic limitations on the interest which can be charged on purchases is needed, so that those least able to make wise decisions in these matters are not hurt.

Local governments should work out ways to permit the gradual accumulation of funds for various projects, and thus stop any unnecessary borrowing. For example, if your school district knows it will have to build a $1 million grade school in five years, there is no good reason why there should be a wait of five years for taxation on such a project. If a small tax could be levied each year before building begins, perhaps $500,000 in bonds will have to be issued rather than $1,000,000—and your district will save hundreds of thousands of dollars in interest.

Economists do not agree on all the causes of inflation, but you do not need to be an economist to know it harms those who can least afford it.

Possibilities for action:

1. When a bond issue is being talked about in your state or community, find out if there are other means of financing a particular need.

2. Do some reading in this complicated field.

3. Check what the legal maximums are for interest in your state, and whether they are excessively high.

6.

When Do You Begin?

This question could be answered in only three letters.

They are: N-O-W.

A decision to do something that is postponed is a decision that is rarely fulfilled. "Some day" is a day that rarely comes.

If you decide to wait to take an active part in political life until after you graduate from college, or until after you are 21, or until after you are married, chances are that you never will participate actively.

Before you begin, however, look at yourself in a mirror. You will see someone with imperfections, who will not always be easy for others to work with. It's important that you recognize this, because when you see imperfections in others it will not turn you aside from what you want to accomplish. You never will be working with perfect human beings.

I do not suggest that you leave school and start a crusade. I do suggest that right this minute, as you read these words, is the best time to decide to do something specific. It may be volunteering in a campaign or it may mean finding out about a problem in your community.

Even if it is a small thing, do it *now*.

Once you sense both the need and the fact that you can be helpful, all of us will be the richer for your experience. Then it is unlikely you will ever stop participating.

"Each time a man stands up for an ideal, or acts to improve the lot of others, or strikes out against injustice, he sends forth a tiny ripple of hope, and crossing each other from a billion different centers of energy and daring, those ripples build a current that can sweep down the mightiest walls of oppression."

—Robert F. Kennedy